What Your Colleagues

Imagine you are climbing a mountain with a large group of people. Hard challenges lie ahead. Now imagine that you have the wisest and most capable, ingenious, clever, and informed trail guide you've ever met at your side, helping you plan and execute your climb. You feel better, don't you? If your "mountain-climb" is redesigning a school to serve students in this vastly challenging world, Grant Lichtman is that guide and this book is your trail map. Don't begin your climb without it.

—Andy Calkins, Director
Next Generation Learning Challenges

It's not enough to build some "new model of education." Change happens faster today than at any other time in history. What we need in education is a cultural and organizational shift that matches the intensity of the future we face. We need a culture of innovation and iteration, where we constantly build, launch, measure, and iterate the best learning and teaching practices we create. In this book, Grant Lichtman has laid out the exact future our schools face and what schools need to do to face this future head on. More than ever, we need a culture of innovation and iteration in our schools, and this book provides you with the tools you need to build and maintain a culture of innovation. Every school leader needs to read this book and use the tools to transform their schools to help students build the knowledge, skills, and abilities to take on the dramatic future they face!

—Jaime Casap, Chief Education Evangelist
Google

Grant Lichtman shares another outstanding book for school leaders, with clear, actionable ideas about how we can get our school organizations to thrive. This is a must-read for administrator- and community-group book studies.

—Dr. Michael Lubelfeld, Superintendent
Co-author, *The Unlearning Leader* and *Student Voice*

In *Thrive*, Grant Lichtman helps us understand that education is at a crossroads in our world. So that our schools do not go the way of the dinosaurs, he lays out the tools we need to manage strategic change and evolve our school systems to meet both the changing needs of our students and the changing demands of our society.

—Dr. Nick Polyak, Superintendent
Co-author, *The Unlearning Leader* and *Student Voice*

Grant Lichtman has done it again, this time setting the stage for one of the most important books for school leaders in our time. Lichtman provides insights and actionable tools for school leaders to navigate the dramatically changing future and role of schools to keep up in the era of school choice and to find relevance in a rapidly changing world. As a principal, this is exactly the type of book our colleagues have been waiting for!

—Dr. Eric Chagala, Principal
Vista Innovation Design Academy

As our society changes, so must our schools. Grant Lichtman has written a necessary book to help schools to develop their road maps to becoming more modern, more relevant, and more powerful places for all who inhabit them.

—Chris Lehmann, Founding Principal and CEO
Science Leadership Academy Schools
Co-author, *Building School 2.0*

In *Thrive*, Grant Lichtman brings together the best minds in education, business, research, history, philosophy, and also the futurists for a dynamic dialogue about "what is possible." If you want to find out what "winning" looks like in school innovation, there isn't a better collection of actual resources or real-time examples than right here! Thank you for making your journey available to all of us Grant!

—Dr. David Miyashiro, Superintendent
Cajon Valley Union School District

Once again, Grant Lichtman uses the power of the keyboard to provoke teachers, school leaders, and policymakers to think differently about schools and, most important, student learning. *Thrive* left me feeling optimistic about what the future of school can be for all students—regardless of school type or zip code—with some easy "next day" strategies alongside some difficult strategic choices that all schools will need, not just to survive but also to thrive in the future.

—Glenn Whitman, Teacher
Co-author, *Neuro-Teach: Brain Science and the Future of Education*

Grant Lichtman has written a powerful book that will help any district or system start to make change. This book will challenge your thinking in a good way. Grant breaks the book down into three sections that help make the material easy to understand. Each section has meaningful tools to help school leaders start to implement changes to impact their students. This should be a book used at the university level to inspire future leaders to enter this profession with a changed mindset.

—Travis Lape, Innovative Programs Director
Harrisburg School District, Sioux Falls, SD

This book comprises the magic trifecta of inspiration, practicality, and a kick in the pants when needed! If you are designing and implementing transformative change in your school, this book is your indispensable source for big ideas, practical tools, and heartfelt inspiration.

—Julie Wilson, Executive Director
Institute for the Future of Learning
Author, *The Human Side of Changing Education*

Thrive

Thrive

How Schools Will Win the Education Revolution

Grant Lichtman

Foreword by Yong Zhao

CORWIN
A SAGE Publishing Company

FOR INFORMATION:

Corwin

A SAGE Company

2455 Teller Road

Thousand Oaks, California 91320

(800) 233-9936

www.corwin.com

SAGE Publications Ltd.

1 Oliver's Yard

55 City Road

London EC1Y 1SP

United Kingdom

SAGE Publications India Pvt. Ltd.

B 1/I 1 Mohan Cooperative Industrial Area

Mathura Road, New Delhi 110 044

India

SAGE Publications Asia-Pacific Pte. Ltd.

18 Cross Street #10-10/11/12

China Square Central

Singapore 048423

ISBN 978-1-5443-8124-4

Publisher: Arnis Burvikovs

Development Editor: Desirée A. Bartlett

Senior Editorial Assistant: Eliza B. Erickson

Production Editor: Amy Schroller

Copy Editor: Amy Harris

Typesetter: Hurix Digital

Proofreader: Rae-Ann Goodwin

Indexer: Judy Hunt

Cover Designer: Scott Van Atta

Marketing Manager: Sharon Pendergast

This book is printed on acid-free paper.

Certified Chain of Custody
Promoting Sustainable Forestry
www.sfiprogram.org
SFI-01268

SFI label applies to text stock

19 20 21 22 23 10 9 8 7 6 5 4 3 2 1

Contents

List of Figures

Foreword

"A model is a nonworking representation of the original." So says Larry Rosenstock, founder of High Tech High, when asked about whether HTH is a model of schools in the future. Larry rejects the idea of finding models to replicate when it comes to creating or improving schools because he believes in the essential role contexts play in making the best schools. The community, the history, the students, the adults, the geography, and the natural and political climate all should shape the school. Thus, all schools should be unique, different from one another instead of being the same.

However, making schools the same seems to have been the dominating strategy for improving education in recent decades. Schools were similar to begin with, but recent educational policies have been pushing schools to become even more uniform and standardized nationally, and even globally, through uniform curriculum standards, standardized testing, and other ostensibly evidence-based policies and practices drawn from flawed international assessments (Schleicher, 2018; Tucker, 2011; Zhao & Gearin, 2016). Even those who wish to be innovative are willing or encouraged to adopt existing models. The growing adoption of the International Baccalaureate (IB) and the franchising of some successful schools is an example (Zhao, 2015, 2016, 2017). Whenever I talk about why we need a new education paradigm, I get asked about whether a model exists. There have not been many attempts to make schools different, although such attempts certainly exist, as my colleagues and I document in our book *From "Yes, But" to "Yes, And": Radical Changes in Education* (Zhao, Emler, Snethen, & Yin, 2019).

It is thus extremely refreshing to read Grant Lichtman's latest book *Thrive*, in which he makes a compelling case for why schools should be unique and different from each other. He argues that for schools to survive and thrive in an increasingly market-driven environment, a school must offer unique values to students and parents. I am no fan of policies that turn education into a free market and use competition to drive educational changes because they often do not work and cause harms (Ravitch, 2010, 2013; Zhao, 2018, 2019). But, I agree with Grant's assessment that schools are not immune to the fundamental change of increasing consumer choices.

What I found most appealing is Grant's call for schools to find their unique value proposition, to find their North Star, and to build a culture of innovations of their own. Schools, not necessarily for the reason to win over other schools, should always be contextualized to meet the unique needs of their communities of students, parents, and educators. Moreover, in a world that needs a new paradigm of education, inventing different alternatives is much more needed than propagating existing models. Learning from others is great, but copying others is not.

In *Thrive*, Grant does a lot more than making the case for unique schools from a business perspective. With his extensive experiences working with schools in different countries and his deep understanding of education, Grant rightly places the human at the center of everything a school does. Naturally, the abundant advice he offers to develop unique schools is deeply rooted in the fundamental respect for all human actors involved in schools.

Such respect is not only necessary for creating winning schools, but also the foundation of true educational excellence.

Thrive goes beyond talking about what we should do; it discusses a lot about how we can do what we should do.

In this book, Grant generously shares his practical wisdom about what works to make schools unique. Drawing from multidisciplinary research and experiences, Grant provides a toolkit of strategies and tactics to school leaders to lead their communities on a journey toward uniqueness. In addition, the book is littered with insightful suggestions for making the journey exciting and rewarding for all involved.

Great schools cannot be copied or franchised. They are invented and reinvented. They are designed and redesigned. I am thankful that Grant Lichtman's book is here to help with the invention and design of unique schools.

—Yong Zhao
University of Kansas

Acknowledgments

I have been fortunate to visit, work with, listen to, and share with so many people, both inside and outside of education, and pieces of those interactions form the spine along which these chapters hang. I have tested and refined what works and what does not with many hundreds of teachers, administrators, students, trustees, and parents; without their feedback, I would be far less confident that these strategies and tactics actually work. Educators beg, borrow, share, and steal from each other, usually with great generosity. I am grateful to all of you!

Along with those specifically named in the book or cited in the references, I want to thank others, some of whom I will surely forget to name, for particularly helping me in my thinking as it has evolved on these subjects over the last 7 to 10 years: Tim Fish and the National Association of Independent Schools Innovation team, Donna Orem, David Monaco and the Center for Transformational Leadership team, Tim Quinn, David Miyashiro, Travis Lape, Mark Siegel, Pam Moran, Joe Erpelding and the entire D39C team, Andrea Fanjoy, Cassidy Lichtman, Julie Wilson, Tom Olverson, the Green Vale School team, The Tilton School team, and the Mt. Vernon Presbyterian School/MVIFI team.

Special thanks to my two partners in the Canadian Association of Independent Schools Strategic Change Accelerator, Justin Medved and Garth Nichols, who have really helped me to refine my thinking about school change processes and both of whom kindly reviewed—and added clarity and content—to drafts of the book.

Special thanks to the team at Corwin and SAGE, including Arnis Burvikovs, Eliza Erickson, Desiree Bartlett, and Amy Harris, for seeing the value in my work and working so insightfully, efficiently, and collaboratively through the editing and production process; and to Andrea Medina who turned ideas, thoughts, and PowerPoint slides into the graphics for the book.

Publisher's Acknowledgments

Corwin gratefully acknowledges the contributions of the following reviewers:

Helene Alalouf
Educational Consultant
New York, NY

Susan Borg
Author, Assistant Professor in
Educational Leadership
The Woodlands, TX

David Horton
Author, Education Consultant
Temecula, CA

Angela Mosley
Administrator
Richmond, VA

Tanna Niceley
Executive Principal, Elementary
Knoxville, TN

Janice Wyatt-Ross
Academy Program Director
Lexington, KY

About the Author

Grant Lichtman is an internationally recognized thought leader in the drive to transform K–12 education. He speaks, writes, and works with fellow educators to build capacity and comfort with innovation in response to a rapidly changing world. Since 2012, he has worked with nearly 200 school and community teams in both public and private schools, helping them to develop their imagination of schools of the future and their places in that future. He is the author of three previous books, *Moving the Rock: Seven Levers WE Can Press to Change Education; #EdJourney: A Roadmap to the Future of Education; and The Falconer: What We Wish We Had Learned in School.*

For 15 years, Grant was a senior administrator at one of the largest and oldest K–12 independent schools in California with responsibilities that included business, finance, operations, technology, development, campus construction, and global studies. Before working in education, he directed business ventures in the oil and gas industry in the former Soviet Union, South America, and the U.S. Gulf Coast. He worked close to center stage in the economic and political transformation of the USSR, the end of the Cold War, and the historic opening of that communist-dominated economy to the outside world.

Grant graduated from Stanford University with a BS and MS in geology in 1980 and studied the deep ocean basins of the Atlantic and Pacific Oceans and the Bering Sea. He and his wife, Julie, live in Poway, California. They have two grown children, Josh and Cassidy, who are doing great things to help improve our world.

Introduction

Sixty-five million years ago, an asteroid roughly the size of Manhattan crashed into the earth with the force of more than a billion Hiroshima-sized atomic bombs. It led to one of the three greatest species extinctions in the history of the planet. In the moments, days, weeks, and decades after the impact, conditions on Earth changed *a lot*. Many species went extinct, including all of your favorite childhood dinosaurs. Even the best, most well-meaning, possibly even "nicest" (in a dinosaur kind of way) Tyrannosaurus Rexes died in the great Cretaceous extinction.

But some species survived. Many animals, plants, sea creatures, and insects we know today somehow made it through that long global winter: crocodiles, sharks, corals, fish, birds, insects, and some little, fuzzy critters that launched the line of mammals from which we all are descendants not only *survived* this great global calamity, but they *thrived* in an explosion of evolutionary success.

Here's the thing: Evolution, either catastrophic like those few years following the asteroid impact or over a much longer period of time, is neither fair nor kind. It is just a force.

During periods of evolution, individuals and species live and die based on their ability to adapt to new conditions. We are currently experiencing a period of global social, technological, economic, and information evolution more rapid than any in the history of humankind. These changing conditions are starting to dramatically impact our systems of education, as families with a radical menu of different options select learning experiences that they think will best prepare their students for a rapidly changing future.

Thankfully, we have not been hit by an asteroid, but the powerful ripples of education innovation are driving some schools toward extinction, threatening the future of others, and creating incredible opportunities for those with vision and courage.

Education is just now starting to feel the impacts of a world of consumer choice. A mere two decades ago, consumers bought what large producers of goods and services told us to buy. Today, around the globe and across virtually every sector of the economy, those tables have turned 180 degrees. Consumers say, "This is what I want, when I want it, where I want it," and producers either create those products and services or they go out of business. This is the evolving world of Uber, not Yellow Cab; Amazon, not Sears; Schwab, not Lehman Brothers; Airbnb, not Hyatt; iTunes, not Sony Records; GrubHub, not Applebee's.

Thankfully, most schools are not for-profit businesses, but schools are *not* immune from this fundamental change. Unlike businesses, many school systems haven't traditionally had to compete for students. Twenty years ago in America, roughly 90 percent of students went to their neighborhood public school. Now that number in some cities and regions is 50 percent and dropping, and in some areas, that curve is steepening, not flattening. And the number of school-age students is falling. Every indication is that in the future both public and private schools will increasingly compete for fewer students who have more choices.

> Every indication is that in the future both public and private schools will increasingly compete for fewer students who have more choices.

If you want your school to survive and thrive in this evolutionary future, you have to understand something that most educators have never had to learn. Marketing guru Seth Godin (2018) puts it in the simplest possible terms: *"The heart and soul of a thriving enterprise is the irrational pursuit of becoming irresistible."*

Regardless of your title at school, you have a role to play in the pursuit of becoming irresistible to families in your community. Your school needs a powerful value proposition that shouts to families, "Pick us!" from all of the options they have. Schools that increase their value proposition over time will have a greater chance of survival; those that fail to boost their perceived value will tend toward failure. We need great schools that provide great learning to not only survive, but thrive.

These impacts are being felt by urban, rural, rich, poor, public, charter, and tuition-charging schools. I have visited and worked with underserved public districts in rural areas where the next school is 40 miles away and school consolidation would mean the loss of a critical community resource. And I have visited and worked with some of the wealthiest, blue-blooded East Coast boarding schools with huge endowments and a long line of students begging to attend. So far, I have not visited a school team that feels 100 percent safe from potential extinction 20 years from now.

Is the problem really this dire? Are some schools really on the verge of becoming extinct? Here are some of the shouts of anxiety, even fear, that I have heard in the last three years at schools just like yours. Have you heard some of them, too?

- "With districtwide choice, families are choosing the magnet schools over our neighborhood school."

- "The private schools are giving more financial aid, and stealing all of our best students."

- "We have always been considered one of the best schools in our city, but we can't compete with online schools that are able to prepare students for the best colleges."

- "The state office is trying to merge our small district with the one in a town 25 miles from here. If we lose our school, we lose one of the few things keeping our town alive."

- "The public schools are providing the same programs we are, and they don't charge tuition."

- "The damned charters are stealing all of our kids."

- "We don't have the resources to take care of kids who live in poverty and struggle to even make it here to school every day."

- "My sister goes to a school where they don't sit and listen to teachers all day. She loves going to school; I want to go there."

- "Some of our teachers split off and created a charter school with exactly our same program, just a few miles away. How are we supposed to compete with that?"

- "We're evaluated by the state on test scores, but our parents and kids don't care about test scores; they want to learn stuff that is going to help them get a good job."

- "We have an incredible reputation, a huge endowment, and our students get into the best colleges, but we're afraid we might not be in business in 20 years."

- "I have one child at a school where the kids are bored and hate going to school and one at a school where the kids are excited and want to stay after school to work on cool projects. Why can't both my kids go to *that* school?"

- "We can't find young people to hire who have the skills we need in today's economy."

I could go on with stories and quotes from parents, teachers, administrators, students, and community stakeholders. You probably have plenty of your own. These are the sounds of schools that have been successful for decades, suddenly finding themselves struggling to compete for students in a time of falling birth rates, vastly greater competition, and a future that is much less knowable than it has ever been in the past. These are the sounds of individuals and perhaps entire species of "school" in the throes of evolutionary selection for which they are not prepared.

Building Hope

There is great news. We know how to deal with these evolutionary pressures. We know how to not only survive but thrive when competition forces or allows us to change. Organizations have been faced with these evolutionary disruptions for centuries. Business schools and bookstores are packed with classes and shelves on how to not only survive but thrive in the face of these challenges. It's likely that neither you nor most members of your school team have taken MBA courses in surviving change and organizational change management, nor do you have the time to read all the books on that shelf of knowledge.

Change means new opportunities to thrill students and their parents. You have the opportunity to connect to your most important purpose, to understand the unique value that you, as a group of passionate educators, can deliver in a way that differentiates you from others. You can understand what families want most and build learning experiences proactively rather than waiting to respond, flat-footed to unpredictable market forces.

And the even greater news? *Your irresistible school of the future is in demand!* It is both needed and wanted by parents and students who know that the traditional school model is not delivering all that they hope for in a school. You can change how your school approaches learning in ways that improve learning for more students! Your "best school" is not a commodity that looks and feels like all others. You can still deliver on what is required by law and college admission offices *and* create something unique that is both educationally profound and attracts families who share your vision. Your school can be the one around which passionate families rally because you have turned a remarkable vision for better learning outcomes into a delivered reality.

Can your school become the one that is attracting more students in this challenging environment? Yes. Is it simple and quick? No. Are there plenty of pitfalls? Yes. Will it work? Yes. Can it lead to better learning outcomes? Yes. How do we know? Because schools all over the country, some of which look a lot like yours, are already on this path.

> Can your school become the one that is attracting more students in this challenging environment? Yes. Is it simple and quick? No.

What This Book Is and What It Is Not

This book is about giving schools the best chance to survive and thrive in periods of rapid evolution, translated specifically for educators. Schools are *not* like Silicon Valley start-ups or big legacy corporations. Schools have special cultures, language, purpose, and conditions. Yet we can learn from those other organizations; the basic rules still apply. This book is the Venn overlap between the best practices of evolving organizations and the realities of running a school.

This book is primarily for school administrators—seasoned, new, and aspirational—who recognize the inevitability of change. Many veteran administrators have spent much of their careers in a time when change was mandated by the Department of Education, not by rising market forces. Newer administrators will be increasingly required to act as effective agents of organizational change as shifting consumer demands and expectations increasingly influence the nature of our schools. Aspirational leaders, that critical cohort of current teachers and noneducators who hope to craft the direction of education in the future, should start practicing these skills by leading innovative change from their own classrooms or offices.

> This book is about giving the best version of your school its best chance to be around for many years, delivering a learning experience that prepares young people for life beyond school. That is the goal.

This book is very specifically *not* about what K–12 learning looks like in the first quintile of the twenty-first century. Many authors have written about, and many educators are delivering every day, what we are starting to see as a student-centered "deeper learning" experience that encourages student ownership of the learning process, inquiry over answers, and interest-based student engagement. Less than a decade ago, when America was at its point of deepest obsession with standardized test scores, schools that offered this pedagogy were viewed as "progressive" or even "quirky." Today, when given some degree of freedom from test-driven learning, many students, parents, and teachers prefer both the process and the outcomes of this deeper learning experience. But not every school community wants to make that shift, and I don't believe there is a single cookbook formula that works for every school. I certainly do not pretend that I know what is in the best interest of the 99 percent of schools that I have not had the honor to visit.

This book is about the *process* of finding and delivering an aspirational value proposition for *your* school; it is not a prescription for what that value proposition should be. This is a book of *practice* that aligns with *theory*. Every part of this book is deeply informed from and by those many dozens of schools I have worked with and those thousands of teachers, administrators, students, and parents with whom I have interacted. These are their stories, their successes, their lessons learned.

> The difference between schools that thrive and those that may wilt or die during this period of evolution is not just about *understanding* how your school can thrive; *it's about actually doing it.*

One of these profound lessons sticks out: *The tools of change are neither difficult to understand nor complicated to implement.* The difference between schools that thrive and those that may wilt or during this period of evolution is not just about *understanding* how your school can thrive; *it's about actually doing it.* It takes time and sustained commitment. That part is up to you.

A short note to non-American educators: While I have worked with schools in Canada, New Zealand, the Middle East and a few in South America, Europe, and Asia, the vast majority of my experience is with American schools. The range of school choice, consumer demand, and educational requirements is different for each country. I hope you will translate or interpolate the examples I give in this book into your own conditions. Having said that, I think there is ample reason to believe that the vast majority of the strategies, skills, and tactics that I offer are *not* American-centric and have been proven to work in organizations across a wide range of cultural and political settings.

The Tools in This Book

The common words that we use and hear—innovation, transformation, personalization, community engagement, marketing, storytelling, strategic planning—are all *processes and tools* we use to achieve that core goal of providing a great learning experience for our students for a long time into the future. The tool kit is robust. Changing an organization such as a school is a complex process. I don't believe we should shy away from complexity with the false hope that tough problems have simple, cookbook solutions. Each chapter is a piece, a tool, or set of tools you can use to help achieve the goal of continuing to serve your community for a long time. Some of these tools come with their own set of helpful metaphors and images; there is no one unifying template I know of that encompasses all of them. That's OK; you will see how the pieces fit together.

The book is broken into three sections (see Figure 0.1). **If Section I**, I define and bring together the three most important concepts in creating long-term success: *value, strategy,* and *innovation*. These are words you have heard loosely bandied about the education world for years. They are powerful words . . . when we know what they *actually mean* and how to use them.

Figure 0.1 The Road Map for This Book

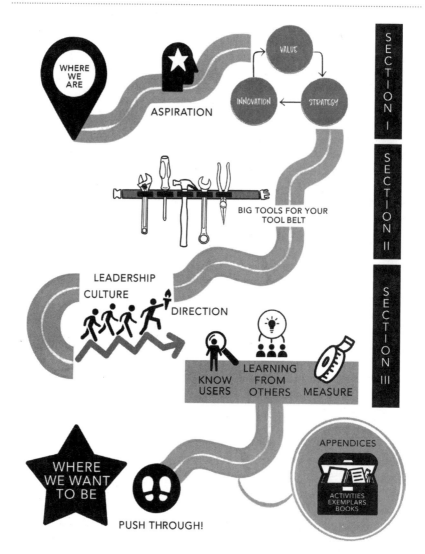

Together, they are the roots, trunk, branches, and nutrients of any organization that hopes to compete and thrive during times of change. Schools have tried over the last few decades to employ these powerful tools. For the most part, we have failed. You can convert that failure to success in your school.

Section II covers what I call the Five Big Tools of strategic change. There are more than this, but these five proven tools are a great place to start. These tools are concrete, relatively simple ways for you and your school team to build both a comfort and capacity for change that can improve learning and create more excitement about what your school has to offer. I know because I have been using them and training school teams just like yours to use them for years. From 2012 to 2018, I have had the privilege to visit and work with thousands of school and community stakeholders at something like 200 schools and districts. I'm the lucky person who gets to see what works, share ideas with colleagues who are creating and testing these tools in their own practices, and test them again and again. I've also had the time to read those shelves of books about innovation, distill the nuggets, try them in real school settings, and share them with you.

Section III deals with the pragmatic reality of how to compete in an evolving marketplace of customers/families who have choices about how and where their kids will be educated. In these chapters, I share what works for schools as well as lessons from other businesses that are very different from schools. We will discuss how you can best understand what your families really want and need; how to align those with practices of great learning; and how to reimagine and reconstruct your school organization to be vastly more comfortable, eager, and able to respond to this crazy, changing world in which we live.

I have included two appendices in this book as well. **Appendix I** is a set of activities in which you and your team can engage to actually *do* what this book describes. These are many of the arrows in my quiver that I use when I workshop with school community teams. Some of these I have borrowed and modified from others; some I have created myself. Some take one minute; some take several months. They work. Cumulatively, these are some of the experiential activities that will help your school to build a comfort and capacity for strategic-level change. There is no formula for when to use each activity, and none is so sacred that it cannot be reimagined by you and your team to fit your particular circumstances. These activities are what build the muscle of the organization, which will not happen if you or a subcommittee try to dictate the steps of change.

Appendix II contains links to schools, networks, and gatherings where education is evolving in America, places and resources where you and your team can start to find and share creative options that might inform your own value proposition, and how to deliver it to your families. This appendix also contains a very brief set of highlights of books that I have read that have contributed to my thinking, that I may or may not have referenced specifically in this book, and that I think you might have not heard about. Some of them are specific to education, but others are very much not specific to education. All of them are good options for summer reading or book clubs with your faculty, administration, boards, and parents.

How Long Does It Take to Transform a School?

The process of change at school rarely follows a linear path, and I don't believe there is a single cookbook recipe that works for all schools. Each school serves a different community, has a different history and culture, has a different level of commitment from leadership, and will come up with different aspirational aiming points. Having said that, I think we are starting to see some boundary conditions to this question.

In 2012, I reported that the evidence showed that for most schools truly significant change could occur over three to five years for the supercommitted and up to 12 to 15 years for schools that took a more hands-off, "organic" approach. Because of a combination of new tools, much greater sharing of ideas, and the emergence of highly differentiated "lighthouse" schools, the pace of potential transformation is accelerating. For example, Harrisburg School District, a suburban district in South Dakota, has developed a remarkable personalized learning track for elementary and middle school students in just three years, and teachers report they are able to completely retool their teaching practice with just six months of training and support.

There are *no longer specific start and end points* to the kind of user-focused, strategic innovation in which schools are now engaged. There is no one point to use each tool in the book, after which it can be put away for years. The process and tools described in this book are the real-life, real-time expression of "growth mindset" that virtually all educators have adopted as a core tenet of good learning. Organizational evolution becomes a state of being; the pace is less comfortable than the relative stasis of the past several decades. That pace must be considerate of the pressures that school stakeholders already feel, but it does not slow down after a strategic planning cycle every five years. The good news is that many of your stakeholders will relish the opportunity to help make your school irresistible.

Exemplar Schools

It is natural that people frequently ask, "What school do you recommend that we visit? Who is really doing it right?"

Ten years ago, there were very few schools in America that were consistently touted as "schools of the future." Several books and even a movie were made about High Tech High, which *is* a great exemplar school, but there just were not many others on the educator's radar screen. Over the last seven years, I have published two books and posted hundreds of blogs that cite well over 200 schools, people, and organizations that might well be viewed as exemplars of school transformation. The schools I cite in this book, including the long list in Appendix II (and many more), are "doing school differently." I feel I have just touched the tip of the iceberg. And I don't pretend to be able to associate any one school with a "thing" that they are best known for. (That would be a full-time job, and the listing would be out of date almost as soon as I made it!) But I do think that these schools provide starting points for you and your team to learn more about the enormous blossoming of educational experiences that are evolving in K–12 today. Reach out to them!

The Sounds Of Schools Thriving

Some schools will make it through this period of evolution; others will not. There are no guarantees during periods of evolution; some conditions are beyond your control. Evolution is about improving the odds, doing everything you can to ensure long-term survival. Evolution is about surviving and thriving in an environment of competition for limited resources.

Some will immediately translate "resources" as money, and they will be wrong. The most critical resource that you need to sustain your school is *students*. With students comes funding. You can have plenty of money, but lacking students, your school will die. If parents and students choose your school or district, you will have the most critical resource you need (though undoubtedly not all that you want). There is only one uber-critical term in this equation: finding, attracting, and retaining families who choose your school in an ever and rapidly diversifying landscape of consumer choice.

> There is only one uber-critical term in this equation: finding, attracting, and retaining families who choose your school in an ever and rapidly diversifying landscape of consumer choice.

So here are the sounds of schools *thriving* that I have heard from people at schools with the *same challenges* as yours, the *same obstacles* to change, serving the *same demographics*, working under the *same laws* and regulations, and in the *same competitive environments*:

- "Once we clearly established who we are and what we are going to be best at, we all had a North Star to align our work."

- "We got out into the community and let them know that 'there is a better way for your child to learn; come see it.' They did."

- "Parents love when their kids are happy and engaged at school. That's where they want to send their next child."

- "We just had to show the community what great learning looks like, and they got it. Parents aren't stupid; they know their children are inheriting a really different world."

- "I get to work on projects that I helped to design and create. When I am doing work at home, it is work I am interested in, not just a set of math problems."

- "When we all got on the same page with a really clear strategy and told those stories every day, our admissions shot up."

- "Most public schools don't do 'marketing'; I hired a marketing consultant to rebrand a school with falling enrollment, and in just the first year, enrollment increased."

- "We were so overwhelmed with other educators coming to see what we were doing differently here that we had to stop informal drop-in tours and set up a couple of days a year to share our story."

- "I've been teaching for 14 years, and I thought I knew my students. I didn't. Now that we have changed to a much more personalized learning system, I really do know my students as individuals; that's why I wanted to be a teacher."

- "If the district decided to backslide on what we have created here, our teachers and parents would file a charter application in a minute. There's no way they are going to let us lose our vision."

You and your school community of stakeholders have a clear choice:

Door A: Bet the farm that this is all wrong. Hope that the world really is *not* changing; that we are *not* in a period of evolution that is powerful enough to threaten your school; that your school, for whatever combination of reasons, will remain immune from the forces of change.

Door B: Convene another strategic planning team that will recommend some modest tweaks to what you have been doing for years or decades and hope that those continue to intersect with future conditions and demands.

Door C: Fight in very positive, fun, engaging, rewarding ways to make your school irresistible!

If you choose Door C, let's roll.

The Road to "Thrive"

Value, Strategy, Innovation

Newton's first law applies equally to physics and organizational dynamics: An object will remain at rest or in uniform motion unless compelled to change by the action of an external force. Due to contrarian forces that have buffeted our schools back and forth, most schools have stayed relatively "at rest" for decades. Now there are new sets of external forces acting on them. Exactly what that new motion will look like, however, is not predetermined for all schools. Schools are people-centric, and people, unlike billiard balls, make choices.

The choice of where you want your school to be in the future starts with understanding your community of users, setting goals, and then willfully, sustainably creating the conditions that move your organization closer to those goals.

If you were operating in a vacuum, if your actions were not impacted by, or had impact on, other people or organizations, that might be enough. But you and your schools are not alone. Your success is a function of two big dynamics beyond the choices you make.

The first is that your school exists to serve others. They also can make choices, and both the number of choices they have and their willingness to make nontraditional choices have exploded in the last two decades.

The second is that the world itself is not standing still. The way students learn, the external impacts on student lives, and the social–economic–technological fabric of student and adult lives are all shifting more quickly than at any other time in human history.

It is the interaction of these three elements—choice, customers, and a rapidly changing world—that demands that effective organizations respond with three powerful instruments of their own: *value, strategy,* and *innovation.* These are what we will gather and unify in the next five chapters.

Schools and communities are not all the same, but we are all living under some shared circumstances. These conditions frame a set of very broadly spaced guide rails for most schools. As you go through this book, don't forget the guide rails in this chapter; they are the context in which we will then develop the key, symbiotic relationship of value, strategy, and innovation.

CHAPTER 1

A Few Big Guide Rails

Before about 2007, most educators had a relatively casual relationship with the changes occurring in the world around us. For most educators, the prevailing attitude was something like, "Yeah, the world is changing, but our mission has not, so please, let me get back to my work."

That started to shift rapidly around 2008 and 2009, for two big reasons. The worldwide Great Recession brought home economic and political realities that most Americans, and many in other countries, had tried to ignore. And emerging, mutually reinforcing technologies allowed an explosion of access to new, competing learning options that challenged the dominance of neighborhood schools. In the last decade, many educators have become increasingly aware that our mission is changing and that they are competing with a lot of other schools for the right to serve students.

The world is becoming increasingly *volatile, uncertain, complex,* and *ambiguous* (VUCA). I find it nearly impossible to argue with this basic premise. Do a web search on the acronym *VUCA,* and you will find that there is a growing universe of ideas around the term, its meaning, and what we are supposed to do about it. Yet when I visit schools, I find that very few people in the room have ever heard the term *VUCA world.* (More on VUCA world at the end of this chapter.) That needs to change. This is our reality and the reality for which we are preparing our students.

As we engage this evolving world where change is rapid and we struggle to predict the future, there are new, basic realities that educators face that have not been uppermost in our thinking in the past. These form the foundation of how schools will operate in the future, if indeed they hope to survive and thrive.

Guide Rail #1: Four Framing Elements to Build Upon

If the world had remained less volatile, and the future relatively predictable, education systems would not be under pressure to change. As you start to build and develop strong, sustainable value for your school or district in this less knowable future, there are four big factors about "change" to keep in mind. These are true for many organizations but are particularly relevant for schools:

1. **Change, in times of evolution, is inevitable**. While all schools will not feel the pace of evolution equally, few will be able to avoid it. You and your school can't choose to live in a less VUCA world.

Every indication is that the magnitude of change is likely to be much greater, happen more quickly, and the results will be less predictable than anything that most of us have experienced in our own lifetimes.

2. **Effective change lies in the alignment of strategy, culture, and practice.** The legendary Peter Drucker famously said, "Culture eats strategy for breakfast." We will mention that quote again in the last chapter, but suffice to say that if strategy, the culture of your school, and the daily experience of your stakeholders are well aligned, it is a good bet that your school's value to the community will rise with the opportunities that change provides and despite the obstacles it presents. If they are *not* aligned, change will likely result in a series of misfires, which will threaten your school's future.

3. **Change requires both comfort and capacity.** For an organization to make significant changes, particularly at the speed that is now required for some schools to maintain or grow their value proposition, stakeholders need to know how to succeed in both their heads and their hearts. They need to *both* embrace the inevitable discomfort of change *and* acquire the skill set of how to ensure those changes create a better learning environment with better learning outcomes for their students. Providing and supporting this *both/and* foundation is the challenging job of leaders during times of change.

4. **Most schools are deficient in "innovation DNA."** When Jeff Dyer, Hal Gregersen, and Clayton Christensen published *The Innovator's DNA* in 2011, they identified five key attributes of people who are effective at leading innovative change: associating, questioning, observing, networking, and experimenting. These do not tend to be skills that are emphasized in schools of education credentialing programs, and they do not tend to be strengths around which many or most educators self-identify. We will go into a sixth characteristic later, risk-taking, that is even more rare within the genetic stew of most schools. This is the hand our schools have been dealt: *We are relatively deficient in innovation DNA.* If change is inevitable, then hiring and fostering educators who are eager and able to be effective innovators is a must. The good news is that many educators are very *willing*—in fact, *eager*—and *more than able* to learn how to become more effective innovators.

Guide Rail #2: The Three Levels of School

In a really macro sense, all schools operate on three levels (see Figure 1.1):

- The top level: "This is who we are and where we're going."
- The middle level: "These systems are in place to help the school to function well and achieve our vision."
- The ground floor level: "This is what we are going to do for and with our students every day."

Figure 1.1   The Three Levels of School That Need to Be Aligned

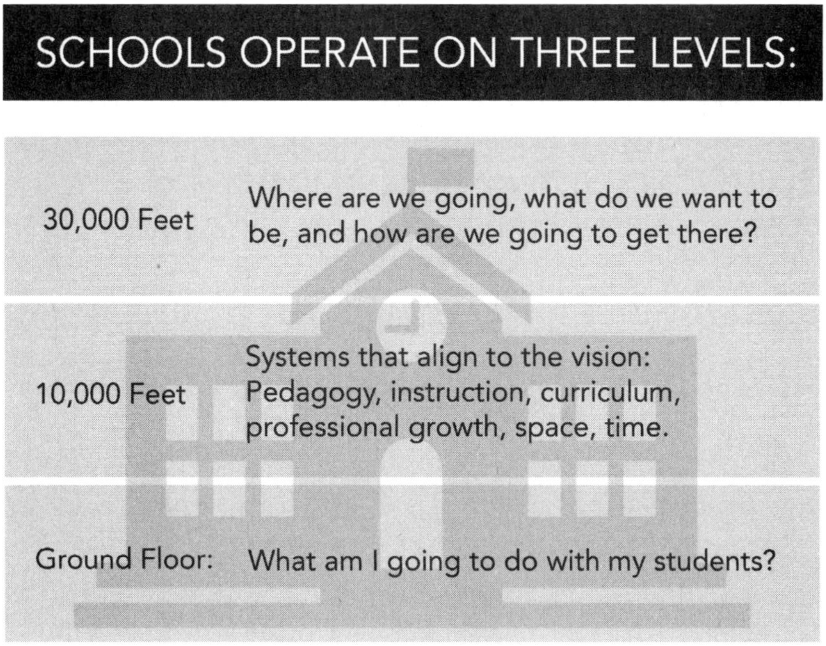

SCHOOLS OPERATE ON THREE LEVELS:

30,000 Feet	Where are we going, what do we want to be, and how are we going to get there?
10,000 Feet	Systems that align to the vision: Pedagogy, instruction, curriculum, professional growth, space, time.
Ground Floor:	What am I going to do with my students?

Schools that work well, and particularly schools that *change* well, are those in which there is close, obvious, clear, frequent, and sustainable alignment across these three levels. As we delve into the tools of value, innovation, and strategy, it will become immediately clear that if many people in the school derive the benefits of this alignment, schools will attract more customers. If these three levels are misaligned, then students and families will not have the daily experiences that they have been promised, and they will look for other options.

In the many schools I have visited and worked with, there is no clearer indication of the thoughtfulness and effectiveness of school leadership than the alignment, or lack thereof, across these three levels. In schools lacking this alignment, the pitfalls are many.

The Pitfalls of Not Aligning Vision to Practice

- The official school vision statement contains promises that are not delivered to students.

- Teachers are unable to deliver on the vision because the school systems do not support their work.

- Classroom practices do not align to the vision.

- District leaders, site administrators, and teachers only see their role as working on one level rather than as part of a team that impacts all levels of the organization.

In well-aligned schools, teachers and administrators, who are the deliverers of the learning experience, **not only *understand* the vision and mission of their school, but they have had a hand in *crafting it*.** And boards or senior administrators who have traditionally been tasked with creating a long-term vision have intimate knowledge of what it takes to actually deliver on those promises.

Guide Rail #3: Two Inescapable Ingredients of Innovative Change

What did fifteenth-century Venetian coffeehouses have in common with Thomas Edison's Menlo Park lab, the World War II codebreakers at Bletchley Park, and happy hour bars in Silicon Valley? All were hubs of dramatic innovation at times when the world was experiencing the social, economic, technical, or political winds of rapid change. And all were filled with the two throughgoing threads that infect organizations that successfully evolve and adapt during such periods: *risk-taking* and *radical networked connectivity*.

Risk-Taking

Making significant change is difficult, if not impossible, without the *willingness to take a risk*. In school terms, what do we mean by *significant change*? Change is relative for each school; I don't believe in one-size-fits-all recipes. But changing a textbook or a curriculum package is not significant. I would argue that a change is significant if it allows or requires the school to change one of the five basic parameters of what I have called the school "operating system."

Examples of Significant Change

1. Changing how time is organized (day, week, month, year)

2. Changing how physical space is used: breaking the boundaries of traditional classrooms and/or static organization of learning space within those rooms

3. Changing how learners are organized (grouping by biological age, subject)

4. Changing the student-to-teacher ratio and relationship; changing the static "one teacher per *X* number of students" for every class period

5. Changing the ownership of learning, from teacher owned to co-owned and student owned.

School communities that accept the challenge of becoming irresistible to their customers/families are willing to take the risk of making changes to one or more of these five elements of the traditional school operating system. First attempts might fail. Successful schools learn from those failures, iterate, and try again because the downside of *not* changing is greater than the risk of shying away from change.

We ask our students to step outside of their comfort zones, to grow as learners every day. We ask them, in other words, to take risks. They watch us; we are their role models. If we are not willing to visibly take risks, why should they? As I discussed in my 2014 book #EdJourney, schools have a special and difficult relationship with risk-taking, but *risk-taking is unavoidable as part of the process of change.*

We ask our students to step outside of their comfort zones, to grow as learners every day. We ask them, in other words, to take risks. They watch us; we are their role models. If we are not willing to visibly take risks, why should they?

The most successful adult risk-takers in schools are willing to expose their own vulnerability, to ask for help as they launch a new unit or practice with an unknown outcome. For teachers, it sounds something like this:

> *"Students, I really need your help. I think we need to try something new. I don't know how it is going to turn out; it might even fail. But together, we will learn more from taking a risk than from avoiding it. We will succeed or fail and learn together. Are you willing to help me?"*

For administrators, just replace the word *students* with *colleagues.*

Risk-taking is infectious. As you will see in Appendix I, there are many ways we can support appropriate risk-taking by just talking about it! What is our understanding of the word *risk*? What level of faith do we have that risk-taking is expected, required, or supported? What pilots are we running or planning for the next week, month, or year? Becoming comfortable with risk-taking in schools is vastly more about the "comfort" than it is about the real risks involved.

Networked Connectivity

The second required pillar of innovative change is *networked connectivity*. As we will see in Chapter 16, having dense, frequent, informative, and diverse connections with people from beyond one's own frame of experience is a key element of change. Hubs of innovation were historically significant because people with different backgrounds and perspectives had a place and time to interact to solve problems of common interest.

One of the biggest mistakes educators make is to visit, watch, and benchmark against other schools that look most like their own. Yes, we can learn from others who are walking a similar path to our own, but historically, innovation has occurred at *the overlap of the known and the less known*, at the margins of our experiences.

In schools, this means getting the heck out of the silos in which most of us spend much of our time. At Design 39 Campus in Poway, the principal really does not have an office; he wants to be present around the school almost all the time. At Mt. Vernon Presbyterian School in Atlanta, and many others, teachers participate in instructional rounds and visit classrooms at a variety of grade levels. Forward-leaning educators visit schools that *don't* look a lot like their own; they participate in Twitter chats and EdCamps to meet colleagues from varied backgrounds; they visit the offices of Google or a local incubator/accelerator in their city. They write blogs and read those of others, and they join book-reading groups about and with not just other educators but thought leaders from across industries so they hear and see about new ideas and trends that will impact their own practice.

Risk-taking and networked connectivity start at the "top" of an organization (I put "top" in quotes because one of the keys to innovative change is distributed leadership structures, and I believe that all educators are leaders. But some have a title that places them "higher" in the school hierarchy). If titular leaders don't set these examples, no one, down to the students, will be as likely to do it on his or her own. Titular leaders absolutely need to figure out how to make connections with "others" fun, expected, required, supported, visible, and celebrated. They are the fuel that drives the engines of innovative change. For some, they are uncomfortable. Great! One of our best measures of innovative change is embracing discomfort.

Guide Rail #4: Living in VUCA World

Throughout human history, the future tended to look a lot like the past. If your parents were farmers, it was a pretty darn good chance that you were going to live your life on a farm, and the methods of successful farming did not change much from generation to generation. A cow was going to still be a cow. Technologies changed at rates that were slow, relative to human life spans. Communication from one part of the world to another took months or years. What we learn about in history—the rise and fall of leaders, empires, and nation states—often had little impact at the local level, except for the endless suffering caused by those ebbs and flows.

This is no longer the case. The speed of change has accelerated to the point that, as Eric Teller of Google X points out, it has exceeded our abilities as human individuals and institutions to adapt to those changes (in Friedman, *Thank You for Being Late*, 2016). Our primary directive as educators is to prepare young people for the future, and that future is less knowable than ever—and becoming *more less knowable* all the time. This is the nature of VUCA world (volatile, uncertain, complex, ambiguous). We don't like it; it can be incredibly uncomfortable, perhaps even frightening, but it is the real world in which we live.

The term *VUCA* arose in the late 1980s within the US military to describe new multilateral global conditions emerging at the end of the Cold War. Now there is an entire industry dedicated to helping businesses, organizations, and people navigate this new normal. VUCA world is different. There is no indication that the curve of change will slow down; in fact, it is accelerating all the time. And there is no "one thing" that educators need to do differently in order to improve. The big problem for educators with VUCA world is that we can't confirm that the solutions we are seeking will actually give us the best results. VUCA by its nature does not allow us to wait for the results of a 20-year longitudinal study. As retired general Stanley McChrystal states in his book *Team of Teams*, "Adaptability, not efficiency, must become our central competency" (McChrystal, 2015).

Very few educators, I would argue, woke up one day when they were 22 or 25 years old, smacked their forehead and shouted, "I REALLY love volatility, uncertainty, complexity, and ambiguity; I think I'll become a teacher!!" Educators generally thrive on predictability and stability; your jobs are hard enough without VUCA in the mix. For decades, the general attitude among educators when faced with change has been "Don't worry; the pendulum will swing back the other way; just wait it out"—and they were usually right.

So what do we do? The best answer is this: In the past, educators have been told, "Stop doing what you have been doing and start doing it differently. We know a better way." In essence, educators for decades have been told to "unfreeze" from their practices of the past and then "move" and "refreeze" as the pendulum of ideas, theories, political leverage, shifting leadership, state and national policies, and sheer hope swung back and forth in the search of improved learning outcomes, whatever we choose that to mean.

In a VUCA world, "unfreeze–move–refreeze" is patently ridiculous because we specifically *don't* know a better way that will *always* be right in a future that is less knowable. The only answer is to become better at, and accustomed to, working in what Gary Hamel and Michele Zanini (2014) eloquently describe as a state of "permanent slush." If you are looking for a great topic for a day of professional learning, start with a community discussion of what "permanent slush" might entail and allow stakeholders to design ways to convert fear of permanent slush into opportunities for dynamic, effective, *fun* growth where the guide rails are less frozen in place.

As we accept that there is a new set of realities, of conditions in the world that we are educating our students to enter, we can now start to build and understand the tool kit we need to help our schools succeed in the future. The remainder of this section is about those tools: *the real definitions, intersections, and power of value, strategy, and innovation.*

BIG QUESTIONS FOR YOUR COMMUNITY

1. How do we actively, frequently, and publicly support risk-takers?

2. How are we connected with "others" in ways that directly help us to evolve as an organization?

3. How are we adapting as individuals and as an organization to the realities of VUCA world?

4. What is our school's appetite for risk, and how do we know this?

5. What is one big risk that our school has taken in the last five years?

*Excitement and enthusiasm are infectious.
Finding and building on that excitement and
enthusiasm are Job #1 in developing a strong
value proposition that will resonate with your
community. If your school's value proposition
is the same as many other schools, why
will families choose you if and when they have
a choice?*

CHAPTER 2

Your School's Value Proposition

All organizations have a value proposition. A strong value proposition is what keeps an organization alive, vibrant, relevant, and sustainably successful. For many for-profit organizations, value is viewed as the long-term usefulness or benefits of the products or services they provide versus the resources required to provide them. By this measure, businesses that create similar products or services at a lower cost have a stronger value proposition than their competitors. Most schools are not businesses, but we still must deliver value to our users.

For decades, many schools, both public and private, did not have to worry much about their value proposition. In America 20 years ago, roughly 90 percent of students attended their neighborhood public school. Many schools provided, by law, similar services. In a given part of cities, schools were more the same than they were different, and in rural areas, there just were no other options. The value proposition of most schools was "We are close by, free, and the law says your child has to attend school," which was enough to keep those schools in business.

Even for nonpublic schools, the value propositions of the few other options open to most families were pretty simple: religious schools offered "an environment that is safer or more controlled than the public schools, with some religious reinforcement"; for independent schools, it was "We are a smaller, safer, more exclusive club where your child will be well known." Even home schooling had a simple value proposition: "You can learn what, when, and how you want."

Thirty years ago, the barriers to competition were steep. It costs *a lot* of money to start a new private school, and no one besides the government could start a public school using taxpayer resources. There were just not many competing choices for consumers. That is no longer the case.

District choice, charter schools, virtual technologies, and an explosion of nontraditional learning options mean that many schools are now competing for students. Even rural schools where there is only one local choice may compete with a school from the next town or with online offerings. In any competitive environment, organizations with a strong, differentiated value proposition survive or thrive; they provide customers a powerful reason to choose

> In any competitive environment, organizations with a strong, differentiated value proposition survive or thrive; they provide customers a powerful reason to choose *their* set of services over all other available choices.

their set of services over all other available choices. Organizations with weak value propositions struggle or fail as their traditional customers go elsewhere.

In my own interactions with school leaders from around the country and across school types, I found that few were thinking about their future as a function of their value proposition prior to about 2012. In 2019, *many* school leaders understand the problem, at least in theory. They recognize that even if the competitive wolf is not at their door today, it very well might be in the near future.

What Is a Value Proposition?

There are many definitions of *value proposition*. The one I like best for schools is this: "Your value proposition is the difference between what you say are going to do and what you actually do, as viewed through the eyes of your customer." It's really quite simple: If customers experience alignment between what you promise and what you deliver, your value proposition rises. If they experience a gap, your value proposition falls.

There are three critical terms in that definition of value:

1. **What you promise.** A strong value proposition requires that the school has and communicates a clear, unambiguous understanding of what it promises to deliver. If the language is wobbly and open to many different interpretations, the value proposition is on shaky ground. Vague, ambiguous statements such as "We have great teachers" or "We value character" are weak pillars upon which to build a strong value proposition.

2. **What you deliver.** A strong value proposition requires that you *actually deliver* what you promise, not just sometimes or for some customers, but a lot of the time for most customers. You can't say you are "a school of innovation where creativity and collaboration are valued" when students spend 90 percent of their day sitting at their desks in rows, listening to a lecture, filling in worksheets, doing predetermined tasks, and answering questions on tests. You can't say your school "meets the needs of individual students" when students spend most of their day in classrooms where all of the students are learning the same things at the same pace.

3. **How the customers view the experience.** To measure or understand movement in your value proposition, you must interact with your customers in ways that allow them to truthfully and fully respond to your proposed value proposition. Schools have a number of customers, or users: Students and parents are the most obvious. But customers/users also include teachers, administrators, other family members, and members of the broader community with whom students and teachers interact.

A (Nearly Universal?) Value Gap

Here is a profound example of a gap between what schools want to deliver and the actual customer experience. I have asked for one-word feedback from thousands of teachers, administrators, students, and parents from a wide range of schools:

"What is one word would you hope that others would use to describe your school? You only get one word. What do you hope this school just 'reeks' of?" The most prominent words generated from these diverse groups from very different schools include *community, curiosity, excitement, passion, enthusiasm, collaboration, inspiring, joy, empathy, engagement, empowered, energy, compassion,* and *connection.*

I then ask high school students and/or their high school teachers: "What is the one word you or your students would use to describe your feelings at the end of a typical school day?"

More than 95 percent give one of three answers (including synonyms): *tired, stressed, bored.* In fact, when I tell an audience, "I will give you four guesses to guess the three common responses," those three words come out so quickly and universally that I rarely have to offer the fourth guess.

This is indeed a profound gap between what we *say* we want and the *actual experience* of our users. Most stakeholders quickly understand that they simply must find ways to align a best version of their school with the actual experience of their key customers. In other words, most of your stakeholders can quickly understand the need to find and deliver a consistent value proposition.

Starting to Build a Winning Value Proposition

Value is not found in a memorable tag line or a new logo. Value is not a brand. A value proposition that will attract families, and on which you can deliver, is not a mission statement that sounds like every other school's mission statement. It is not the nuts and bolts of your curriculum, your school history, or your campus master plan. It starts, as Seth Godin says, "with dreams and fears, with emotional states, and with the change your customers seek."

A winning value proposition has nuance; it is different from others'; it has clear purpose, defined in words that your community understands and will rally around. I like to have school stakeholder groups start to think more deeply about their winning value proposition using three elements:

- What are the **guiding lights** toward which your school will move?

- What are the **fence lines**—the nonnegotiables—beyond which your school will not stray?

- What are the **colors** of your value—the adjectives, adverbs, programs, and daily experiences—that will differentiate what you do well from what other schools do well?

Guiding Lights

Just as Dorothy knew that the first step toward the Emerald City started at the beginning of the Yellow Brick Road, it is imperative that an organization have a destination in mind before it begins the process of innovative change. In Chapter 12, we will dig down on this, creating a North Star for the school or district, but early in the process, it helps to not limit your thinking, trying to find that "one great goal" that will create value in the eyes of your customers. Rather, imagine a set of targets around which you will create your strategies. So we ask this question: *What are some aiming points that reflect the best version of our school in 10 to 20 years?*

In diverse teams of stakeholders, brainstorm answers to this open-ended question. It will be easy to create lists with ill-defined words; the less well defined, the less we really have to struggle with what implementation will *actually* require! Here are some examples of poorly worded goals and their better-alternative guiding lights:

> **Poorly Worded Goal**: *We will hire and retain excellent faculty.* What does the word *excellent* actually mean? Is your school ready to write a rubric for "excellent" when it comes to teachers, just as we do for student performance in our classes? If so, this is a great guiding light; if not, it is a meaningless platitude.

> **Good Guiding Light**: *We will create a clear set of objectives and expectations for what it means to be a great teacher at our school. We will hire faculty who understand and embrace those expectations, and hold themselves accountable.*

> **Poorly Worded Goal**: *We will offer a rigorous academic program.* What does *rigorous* mean, and compared to what?

> **Good Guiding Light**: *Our course offerings and assessment standards will allow our students to be viewed favorably by a wide range of colleges and universities, including the most selective.*

> **Poorly Worded Goal**: *We will be the best school in our city (or region or state)* or *We will be recognized as a national thought leader in education.* What do *best* and *leading* mean? In what ways will those labels be applied and meaningful?

> **Good Guiding Light**: *We will have the highest test scores among schools in our region with similar demographics* or *We will become a destination school where other educators visit on a weekly basis to learn about how we learn.*

Fence Lines

In any good learning or design experience, we have to recognize some boundary conditions beyond which it is not useful to stray. We want to encourage creative thinking and innovative solutions, but if we do not honor certain fence lines, we run the risk of creating solutions that are not possible, let alone probable. So we ask this question: *What are the nonnegotiables or boundary conditions beyond which our strategies should not stray?*

For various schools, some of these fence lines might sound like the following:

- "We will not move our physical campus from its present location."

- "We will remain a (fill in the blank here) single-gender, faith-based, boarding, charter, free public school."

- "Our student body will closely reflect the social, economic, racial, and ethnic diversity of the community we serve."

- "The arts will always play a leading role in what and how we learn."

- "We will embed elements of social and emotional wellness learning in every aspect of the student and teacher experience at our school."

The fewer fence lines, the more flexibility the school has in defining and delivering a winning value proposition. But if we ignore critical fence lines at the outset, then the resulting value proposition might be unrealistic, undeliverable, or less irresistible to our customers.

Colors

Think about your school's value proposition like a painting. The guiding lights are elements of the vision you have before you start to draw; you are asking, "What do we want this picture to look like way in the future, when we are done?" The fence lines are like the sketch that a painter lays down on the canvas—the basic framework of the painting before it really evolves. Once we have those, we can start to add the colors that will turn the canvas from a stretched fabric with a set of lines into a unique painting. So we ask this question: *What are some of the elements of the school in the future that will clearly differentiate us from other educational options, some of which we don't even know about today?*

Adding color is both the most fun and the most challenging step of imagining a winning value proposition. You can brainstorm all kinds of programs and opportunities you want to offer your families, teachers, and students. But a school simply can't be all things to all people and hope to survive. We have to make choices—not because we value one learning outcome or one set of student interests more than another, but because no school can afford to be all things to all people. *Effective organizations don't have multiple value propositions.*

> We have to make choices—not because we value one learning outcome or one set of student interests more than another, but because no school can afford to be all things to all people. Effective organizations don't have multiple value propositions.

Some examples of "colors" that start to fill in the painting of a school's winning value proposition might look like these:

- "We will be a [fill in the blank: STEM, art, language, business skills] magnet school; we will offer all subjects to the degree that they are required for graduation and college acceptance, but students will come to us primarily because their passions align with [fill in the blank]."

- "Our students will be able to create their own learning pathways; our daily schedule and program offerings will be structured to give students the maximum flexibility possible in creating an individualized learning path."

- "We will provide opportunities for students to prepare equally for vocational and higher education opportunities beyond graduation."

- "Our school will be a place where students and faculty focus on human interactions in a world that is becoming increasingly depersonalized through the use of digital technologies."

Once a community of school stakeholders has had the chance to create expansive lists of options in these three categories, and once they have drilled down to the real meaning of the words they want to use, the school is ready to make some big, and often difficult, choices. Think about the struggles that a company such as Apple went through before landing on a product like the iPhone. What is more important: portability or a large screen? Do we want users to interact with a finger or a pointing device? What kind of software system do we build? What about shape, color, and price point?

Successful organizations have to "double down" on some choices and abandon others, and they are not always correct in the choices they make. As we will see in the rest of this book, successful organizations learn to rebound from failure, to not put all of their bets on a single square, and to create strategies that allow for flexible innovation. But flexibility does *not* mean all choices are equal or that generalities are as valuable as specifics. Value is about finding a set of common goals, committing to them, and then delivering on that commitment.

BIG QUESTIONS FOR YOUR COMMUNITY

1. What is our value proposition? How do we know that it aligns with the values of our community? Can we all articulate it?

2. How is our value proposition clearly differentiated from that of other nearby schools that might be an option for our families?

3. How do we know if we are delivering on our value proposition?

Value is not found and delivered by accident.
Finding, creating, and codifying a truly
strategic pathway that captures both the
obstacles and opportunities facing your school
community is Job #2 in delivering on a strong
value proposition . . . which leads to continued
demand for your school.

CHAPTER 3

What Is Strategy?

Even a few decades ago, few schools had anything that resembled a strategic plan. Starting in the 1980s and 1990s, planning and acting strategically became a standard best practice for schools. Public districts, often mandated by state regulations or federal funding incentives, began to create annual or multiyear goals against which their progress could be measured. Private schools created five-year plans that set targets for things like hiring, diversity, technology adoption, building plans, raising money, and tuition rates.

Some schools today still do not develop long-range plans. They work each year as they did the last, and are largely *reactive* to changes in their market or the shifting demands sent down from state or federal regulators. Having no road map for the future is, at best, a recipe for mere survival. Having a plan, any plan, around which a school system can agree and work toward common goals is almost always better than having no plan at all.

Having said that, the vast majority of school strategic plans I have seen share one thing in common: *They are not strategic at all.*

Strategy is, simply, about *making choices that give your school or district the best opportunity to thrive* in the future. That is where we have to start.

Every organization that lives in a competitive marketplace has just two "keys to sustainable success," according to strategy guru Michael Porter (1996): good strategy and highly effective operational systems.

- *Effective strategy* means that you are delivering different services from your rivals or that you are performing those core services in demonstrably different ways.

- *Operational effectiveness* means that your school is better at delivering your core service—in this case, learning—than are your competitors.

For decades, schools have delivered services that were quite similar. Even between public and private schools and those serving different social and economic demographics, the similarities among schools have been much greater than the differences. School managers relied almost exclusively on operational effectiveness—"We are doing it better than they are"—using industry benchmarks such as test scores, graduation rates, college matriculation statistics, and parent surveys as measures of success.

There are a number of problems that arise from relying on operational effectiveness as a key to sustainable success. One is that schools *want* to look like each other; we measure ourselves, and are measured by others, against other schools. The problem with that is, as Porter points out, "The more companies benchmark, the more they look alike," and in a differentiating marketplace, looking the same is not your goal.

The biggest problem, though, is the simplest: Educators love to share, so best operating practices spread rapidly, leaving leaders with no competitive advantage. Nearly every school I visit, for example, feels that the most powerful and unique elements of its learning experience are the "relationships" that students have with "quality" teachers and other students. We know that relationships and good teachers lead to good learning results, but if many schools offer these, then good relationships and quality teachers are not a *differentiating* advantage.

The only other route to long-term success for schools, both public and private, that find themselves in increasingly competitive marketplaces lies in effective strategic positioning. "Competitive strategy," says Porter, "is about being different. It means deliberately choosing a different set of activities to deliver a unique set of values." Not *everything* a school does has to be different in order to offer a strategic advantage. Every school may, for example, offer courses that fulfill college admissions requirements and assess students according to a common set of standards. But successful schools increasingly figure out what else they can offer, or offer in a different way, that resonates with what *their* community wants and needs.

> Educators love to *agree and include*; it is uncomfortable for us to *disagree and exclude*. Yet strategy requires that we make these choices; we simply cannot be great if we try to be great at everything.

Porter resurrects ancient wisdom when he reminds us that "the essence of strategy is choosing what *not* to do." This could have been lifted straight from Sun Tzu's fifth-century (BCE) treatise *The Art of War*—"The best battles are the ones we don't fight"—or from Laozi's fourth-century (BCE) work *Tao te Ching*: "To attain knowledge, add things every day; to attain wisdom, remove things every day." Educators love to *agree and include*; it is uncomfortable for us to *disagree and exclude*. Yet strategy requires that we make these choices; we simply cannot be great if we try to be great at everything.

A good strategic plan, or what I hope will become a *process of strategic design*, should focus on generating answers and ongoing iterations to Lafley and Martin's (2013) five-question strategy rubric (see Figure 3.1). A good strategic plan can have just these five major headings. At a minimum, every major goal of a good plan will *clearly* relate to answering one of these questions. Everything else—all that follows—is tactics. Tactics are *really* important, but as we will see in Chapter 5, they exist to support strategies.

Figure 3.1 The Strategy Rubric

Strategy for schools boils down to a few essentials. Let's start with what strategy is *not*:

Strategy is *not* . . .

- **A short vision statement** that usually sounds a lot like that of many other schools and is filled with words and phrases that, although lofty, are ambiguous.

- **A plan.** Having a plan does not mean that it is being implemented, and strategy *must* be implemented or the planning is a waste of time.

- **Optimizing the status quo.** If your school is already so good and your view of the future so clear that status quo is the best option, you don't need a new strategy. For most organizations experiencing a period of evolution, status quo means you are probably falling behind others that are innovating for the future.

- **Following "benchmark best practices."** There are reasons to benchmark against other schools, and they are almost universally tactical. Creating a *strategy* based on best practices is almost a guarantee that your school will *not* be uniquely positioned because benchmarking is based on averages of what other schools are already doing, and "average" is rarely a winning aspiration.

In their widely followed primer on strategy, *Playing to Win* (2013), A. G. Lafley and Roger Martin lay out their Five Questions of Strategy model, a simple rubric that defines what strategy really is, stripped of all platitudes and mythology:

1. **What is our winning aspiration?** What is it that will set your school apart from other learning options for families? Is it truly aspirational? Will it excite people to rally to your flag? (Educators sometimes shy away from the term *winning*, but in this context, it merely means thriving in the future.)

2. **Where will we play?** What is your market; who are the families you are trying to attract? Where do they live, and what other options do they have? Every marketplace is unique, and knowing the market—what Sun Tzu (2003) calls "knowing the ground"—is critical to developing winning strategies.

3. **How will we win?** What will your school do better than others who are "playing" in the same market? Why will it be better in the eyes of your stakeholders? How will you clearly differentiate your services and outcomes well enough that you will consistently and sustainably fill your seats?

4. **What capabilities must we have to win?** *How will you actually deliver* on your aspirational promise? How will you align pedagogy, curriculum, time and space, professional learning, class offerings, communication, and human resources in clear, direct support of your aspirational vision?

5. **What management systems do we need** in order to ensure effective implementation of our strategy and tactics? How will you measure effectiveness to know if you actually *are* winning?

Does Your School Need Strategy?

Organizations are all unique. They have different starting points, different histories, and serve different customers. These differences mean that they can, and often must, approach strategy from different points of view. There are at least three factors that can influence how an organization views the need for true strategy. I don't think that these factors *should* influence the approach to strategy, but pragmatically, they probably do:

- **Birth**: Unfortunately, people are not born with equal power to influence their futures, at least not in most of the world. All data suggest that race, gender, socioeconomic status, parents, and geography are powerful positive boosters or heavy weights on individual aspirations. The same is true for organizations. Schools have very different "birth points" when it comes to future success. Some start with distinct advantages of resources, geography, demographics, ideas, and human capital. I wish this were not so, but I am a realist. The more a school community believes that its "birthright" is inviolate, the less it will feel the need to dig into real strategic thinking.

- **Luck**: Some people and groups seem to get all the luck. They intersect the right places at the right times—not because they have a crystal ball or a great reason to do so, but because statistically *someone* has to be the lucky winner! Should we rely on luck to help us mold the future? Should we place our faith in the statistical probability that we or our school will have as much good luck as bad? Does it help to pray for good luck or the intercession of a higher power? For some, luck and faith are good and effective ways to influence a future, and I won't argue that they are always wrong. If a school organization has been lucky in the past, there is a tendency to think that good luck is enough for the future.

- **Pounce**: Some people and groups create their futures by capitalizing on circumstances. The most effective natural predators react quickly and powerfully to the opportunity of a meal. The most effective prey respond just as quickly to dangers. Neither mentally map out each of those changing conditions, but the best are better when it comes to reacting to changes in the world around them. They are the first to see opportunities and dangers, gain the advantage of speed, and can be remarkably successful as long as their instincts continue to serve them well. Organizations that are effective at "pouncing" may think that intuition is enough of a guide for future success.

Strategy is about proactively and consciously devising a set of steps that increases your chances of winning. Strategy has no place in a pure-luck game of cards. But strategy and to some extent "pouncing" have everything to do with winning at a game of chess or *Go*. These can improve, though not guarantee, the chances of winning, even if an organization is not "born" with advantages or does not intersect success via pure luck.

Does every school need a strategy? The more you can truly rely on the strength of your legacy, your belief in luck, and your ability to pounce at the right time, the less strategy you need. The converse is also true. Good leaders are generally unwilling to bet the farm that things such as history, legacy, and luck are guarantees of future success.

BIG QUESTIONS FOR YOUR COMMUNITY

1. How does our current strategic plan measure up against the strategy rubric in this chapter?

2. What are three other "competing" schools in our area? How is our value proposition different from theirs? How are we doing relative to them in ways that matter most to us?

3. What have we chosen to *not* do that other schools are still doing?

4. How might we move forward with an inclusive approach to answering the five questions that define real strategy?

5. How, and how often, do we get out into the community to measure its needs and wants?

With even the start of a winning strategy, schools ask, "What do we need to do to go from where we are to where we want to be?" Keeping what is most valuable, and changing what needs to be changed, is Job #3 in beginning to deliver on a strong value proposition . . . which leads to continued demand for your school. Innovation is, simply, making those changes.

CHAPTER 4

Innovation

The Link Between Value and Strategy

We have defined *value*: promising and delivering what your customers want and need.

We have clarified *strategy*: making choices that enable your school to continuously deliver on a winning value proposition.

Now we can link these together in the very real world where the demands we face are changing *and* other schools are competing with yours to attract customers who have more choices than they have had in the past.

When the competitive marketplace, or the world in general, is *not* changing much, organizations look for small operating efficiencies in order to be "better" in the minds of their customers. Are there *real* differences between two types of laundry soap? Between Ford and Chevy trucks? Can most consumers *truly* tell the difference between Bud Lite and Miller Lite in a blind taste test? This has been the field of play for schools for decades; most schools looked pretty much the same, and that was OK.

But that is no longer the case. The world demands that we prepare students differently, and providers of those differences are charging onto the field.

What Is Innovation?

For at least the last 500 years, organizations that have succeeded in turbulent times are those that have been the most "innovative," a descriptor that is thrown around as much as any in this first quintile of the twenty-first century. But what does it actually *mean* to be an innovative school, and how does innovation create and amplify value-boosting strategies for your school?

Am I an innovator if I do something differently today than I did yesterday? Is my team innovative if we use lots of sticky notes or collaborate on a whiteboard? Is my school innovative if we use laptops in class or teach our students to code in elementary school? Do I have to invent something that radically changes the way humans work or play to be considered an innovator? Do I, in the oft-cited language of Clayton Christensen, have to "disrupt" a sector of commercial markets with a product or service that fundamentally changes how people lead their lives?

What does innovation actually mean *for schools*? This was the question I set out to answer as I drove around the country in my Prius for three months in the fall of 2012, visiting 64 schools in 89 days and interacting with hundreds of school stakeholders. A key takeaway from that unique look at schools (*#EdJourney*, 2014) was that most educators, when asked about the word *innovation*, immediately defaulted to something related to technology. Fortunately, that is changing; we are starting to understand what innovation in schools actually means.

As with "value proposition," there are many definitions of "innovation." There are entire bookshelves dedicated to the process of innovation, but this is the scaffold that I think works best for schools:

- Innovation is *not* about technology.

- Innovation is *not* about ideas.

- Innovation is *not* even about *good* or *great* ideas; schools are *full* of wonderful people with great ideas. (How often have you heard someone propose something new to the school and the response from someone else is "That's a great idea!"?)

- *Innovation is about creating, finding, and implementing new ideas that add value to the organization in the long term.*

We have already seen that every school community has a value proposition that they try to uphold, both because they believe in the critical importance of education and because they want their school to thrive. Anyone who helps build on that value proposition is a potential innovator. An idea for a new program, practice, or process that will strengthen that value proposition is potentially innovative. Not all of these ideas will work, but we only know if we test them, learn from the failures, support the early successes, and leverage what we learn in the process.

There is real power in the process of innovation; there are also real traps. I have visited too many schools that shove a shelf of Legos and a 3-D printer into a corner of the library, call it a "makerspace," and point to it as an example of innovation. I have had calls from schools that laboriously rebuilt the daily schedule only to come up with one that is about 80 percent the same as the former schedule and does little to change how learning *actually* takes place. I visit schools all the time that proudly lead me through pretty new buildings that are light and airy, and I still see class after class of disengaged students sitting in rows of desks, listening to a teacher lecture in front of a PowerPoint presentation.

I have also visited schools where *real* innovation is taking place, where a teacher is testing a new unit, boosting engagement with student-centered pedagogy, empowering students to ask deep questions, or using the campus beyond her or his classroom as a learning laboratory. I have seen teachers learn with colleagues from another school they will never physically visit and then share what they learned with other teachers on their own campus. I have watched teachers develop a pilot project with a team of other teachers and students, launch the pilot in September, and then redesign it for the following year. Most importantly, I have watched teacher innovators stop "doing for" their students, back off, and let student innovators do and learn for themselves.

Most of these innovations don't dramatically change the school overnight. Many of them occur in a single classroom or among a team of like-minded colleagues. They share one strength: These *potential* innovations, if nurtured and spread across the school, can lead to real value enhancement.

They also share one great weakness: They are often unknown even by colleagues teaching in the next hallway. This is the real challenge of "innovation" for schools: You have to know it, mean it, champion it, nurture it, live it, and tell the story, or innovation just becomes another swing of the education pendulum, which we all know has no beneficial momentum of its own.

The Value–Strategy–Innovation Flow

We now have the three key definitions we need to help your school intentionally develop and deliver on a winning value proposition:

- Value as viewed through the eyes of the customer

- True strategy

- Innovation

We need innovation in our schools in order to add value, to keep improving our services so our customer/users (parents, students, teachers, community stakeholders) keep coming through our doors and supporting our work. And in order to do *that*, we need strategies that promote value-building innovations (see Figure 4.1).

This flow lies at the core of strategic change. It allows us to sort out truly strategic, value-building innovation from all of the chatter—the hundreds of

Figure 4.1 The Value–Strategy–Innovation Flow

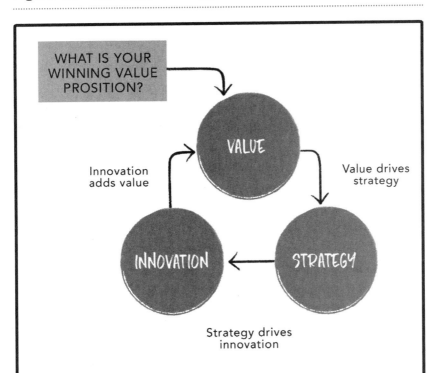

new curriculum packages, teacher training videos, cool new technologies, time tweaks, flavor-of-the-month and must-have programs, and the rest of the waterfall of stuff that is constantly pushed at all educators under the guise of "this is *really* going to positively change how your students learn." Is there value in some of that cascade? Of course! But all of that is servicing a very tactical level of your school. Most of it will *not* build long-term value because the "next best thing" is going to be pushed at you and your colleagues next year at the annual conference you attend or next week on your web feed, and other schools are going to offer those new flavors of the month as quickly as they can.

Think about it this way:

- Tactical improvements in operating efficiencies are like the leaves on a tree: very important, but they come and go (see Figure 4.2).

- Value is like the branches. Even if the tree is bare in winter, we see the reach and breadth of the tree. Branches of value are permanent places for those operating tactics to grow.

- Strategy is like the trunk. With a strong, healthy trunk, trees can afford to lose a few limbs; without a strong core, the tree falls down.

- Innovation is like the roots, finding and providing new sources of nutrients that will ensure good growth in the long term.

Figure 4.2 The Thriving Tree

And this is *really* important: *Strategy is not something that just "leaders" use and worry about!* The value–strategy–innovation equation is important at all levels of a school and at all scales. It not only works, but it is needed—in grade-level and department planning as much as it is at the division, site, and district levels. As I said in the introduction, this book is not just for leaders with lofty titles. If our schools are going to change, it will be because we empower and train all of our educators to understand and help to implement this value–strategy–innovation flow.

BIG QUESTIONS FOR YOUR COMMUNITY

1. What jumps to mind when we use the word *innovation*?

2. How is your school innovating in ways that don't revolve around a new technology?

3. How do innovations at our school lead to greater value, or do we innovate for the sake of innovating?

4. How are we being intentional about innovation at our school?

5. Who is responsible for being innovative at our school? Who are our lead innovators?

By definition, value-building innovation is not handed down from above. Building a community that has a hand and a stake in asking the really big questions and creating its own future is Job #4 in beginning to deliver on a strong value proposition . . . which leads to continued demand for your school.

CHAPTER 5

Shifting From Strategic Planning to Strategic Design

Our world moves too quickly for infrequent attention and rigid thinking. The changes in what we know about how children learn, how the brain works, new technologies, and the impact of social media (such as high–screen time addictions) are so significant that they have to be reflected in near-real time if we hope to continue to deliver relevant learning in our schools. If we hope for our students to learn how to work effectively in an increasingly VUCA world, we certainly have to model a creative, nimble approach to how we imagine the best futures for our schools.

I have looked at *a lot* of school strategic plans in the last decade, and many of them share some unfortunate characteristics:

- **They are not actually strategic**. As we discussed in Chapter 3, most plans are almost completely *tactical*. Tactics are extremely important, but they are not strategies. We will sort out the differences in this chapter.

- **They are way too long**. We create these plans with diverse groups of stakeholders, and we don't want to make anyone angry or feel left out, so we include long lists with little filtering or prioritization. I have read five-year strategic plans with a dozen big "strategies" (which are not actually strategic) and more than 100 underlying implementation tactics and goals!

- **They are inward and backward looking**. What they really say is "We have studied what we have been doing at our school, and here is how we are going to do it better." They focus on your own school's performance and can ignore the really big changes in the world around you. They use the past as the primary guide to the future, which, by definition, is dangerous in VUCA world.

- **They look at the short and medium term**, which is a double whammy for schools. Five years goes by in a snap in schools, yet many of the changes confronting schools happen in time frames much faster than five years. I like to remind educators that 10 years ago we were teaching second graders how to "keyboard" (the modern form of typing class that I took when I was in high school). Just a decade later, second graders may be designing and printing prosthetic hands! Schools should have a longer *strategic* time horizon (10–20 years) and a more dynamic, fluid, nimble ability to rethink *tactics* as conditions change.

- **The work is the responsibility of a relatively small committee**. The committee seeks input from a broader group of stakeholders, but the larger community rarely digs deeply into both the opportunities and inevitable obstacles of real strategy. Most stakeholders have little skin in the game, which means they don't really own implementation of the results.

- **They are not differentiated**, which means they are not truly strategic. Most strategic plans I see fall into one of two categories: "vanilla" (looks almost exactly like every other school's strategic plan) or "vanilla plus" (has a couple of interesting elements that are potentially differentiating but is swimming in a sea of sameness). School communities that really understand strategy will at least consider a "Cherry Garcia" plan!

We are starting to see a convergence of school communities that are taking a very different approach to strategy. With intentional reference to the process and tools of design-based thinking, I call it *strategic design* rather than strategic planning. At schools that are taking this approach, the process of developing strategy looks much more like what you see in Figure 5.1.

Figure 5.1 What Strategic Design Looks Like

- **The focus is on true strategy**. School communities distill large volumes of value-rich aspirations from their community down to a few core strategies that focus on the key questions of gaining, winning, measuring, and managing a long-term value proposition.

- **The resulting plans are short**. The community forces itself to prioritize and make choices. They don't create long lists of goals just to please everyone, knowing that they can't do it all.

- **They are outward and forward looking**. The community members honor and reflect on the past, but they are not *constrained* by it. They look to other schools that are very different from their own and to the much broader world to understand future challenges. In military language, they focus on fighting the next war, not the last one.

- **They look way beyond the next five years**. They push their community to consider what is likely or inevitable, even in a less knowable world, 10 to 20 years from now.

- **The process is not limited to a five-year cycle.** They find ways for strategic and tactical discussions to permeate the organization. They frequently discuss strategy, which evolves organically as the school adapts innovative tactics to meet changing needs.

- **The entire community "owns" strategy**. Using good design-based practices, large, diverse groups engage in frequent, often short, conversations. The process is highly inclusive and radically transparent; all members of the wide school community both contribute to the creation of strategy and have access to what other stakeholders think.

- **The process is less linear, more ongoing, and messier** than traditional strategic planning processes. As with any good learning, it tends to be noisy and a bit chaotic. There are not always clear start and stop points in how the community manages its strategic trajectory.

- **The deliverable is not a static plan, but a truly strategic road map**, subject to modifications. It is "more different" than other schools' plans. It tells the community, "This is where we are going, so if you like it, choose us. If you don't like it, choose another option that is right for you."

Strategy and Tactics

Real strategies directly answer one of the five questions in the Lafley and Martin (2013) model. Strategies serve to deliver on your highest aspirations. As we said earlier, strategy is the trunk of the tree; tactics are the small branches and leaves. Strategies are subject to change, but not often and only when you have indication that the strategy is failing. Tactics are subject to much more frequent iteration.

Good *strategies* are tied directly to the Five Questions of Strategy model (p. 23). Good *tactics* are tied back to one of those *strategies*. Both are important, but we should never focus on tactics until we have clarified the strategy they will support. It is a simple cart-and-horse exercise to make sure you have well-articulated strategies before focusing on tactics.

Here are some examples:

Strategy: Our school will be the local leader in modern STEM education. (This answers Strategy Question #1: What is our winning aspiration?)

Tactics:

- Hire faculty who have specific track records in developing and delivering interdisciplinary STEM instruction.

- Develop and implement a communications plan that builds the school's STEM reputation across the community and in the region.

- Create a system of tangible rewards for faculty who create and sustain new programs that advance STEM learning.

Strategy: Our school will offer personalized learning to all students. (This answers Question #3: How will we win the market?)

Tactics:

- Hire faculty who are eager to grow professionally and are willing to be flexible in how and what they teach.

- Rebuild the daily schedule to allow more flexible times for personalized learning experiences.

- Research options for classroom furniture pieces that promote personalized learning and allocate resources to classroom renovations.

The concept of strategic design encompasses the entire spectrum of practice and activities in this book. Good strategic design does not start on one day and end when a plan is adopted. All of the big tools of strategic change that we will discuss in the next section are part of ongoing strategic design. Strategy is not a *thing*; it is a *process*. The adjectives I use to best describe a good process of strategic design are *highly aspirational, radically inclusive, overly transparent, uncomfortably ongoing,* and *a bit messy.*

> Strategy is not a *thing*; it is a *process*. The adjectives I use to best describe a good process of strategic design are *highly aspirational, radically inclusive, overly transparent, uncomfortably ongoing,* and *a bit messy.*

If diverse groups of stakeholders are involved in designing strategy, they will be much more invested in developing and actually implementing the tactics to make the strategies succeed. It is the role of governing boards to *approve* strategy and to hire a chief executive who will *implement* it. Tactics are owned by the professional administration and the teachers, not the school board or trustees.

Strategic *plans* tend to be long and dusty; most school stakeholders have no idea what is in them or how they are supposed to personally contribute to the broad plan goals. Strategic *design* is *personal*; more people's hands are dirty from the process, which means there is more personal buy-in and understanding. The plan was not handed down from "them"; it came from "us." Humans are much more likely to agree to embrace the inevitable discomfort of change if they see their own voice and choice in at least some part of that change.

BIG QUESTIONS FOR YOUR COMMUNITY

1. How does our strategic plan take into account what other schools are doing and the changes in the world outside of education?

2. Who had real, thoughtful input into your strategic plan?

3. Which of the main headings in our current strategic plan are actually strategic, and which are tactical?

4. How are all of the strategies and tactics we are pursuing connected, and are they connected to a major aspirational goal?

The Five Big Tools of Strategic Change for Schools

In the first section, we developed the argument that sustainably successful schools will have powerful aspirations that overlap with those of the community they serve. They will align strategies and practices of innovation in order to deliver on those aspirational promises. All of that is the first, critical step. Now we have to face the inevitable questions: *How do we get from where we are to where we want to be? How do we actually change a school, a district, or a culture with the resources and commitments we have and in a time frame that is relevant to our students?* How to change a school or district is the subject of this section.

Changing a school culture and practice is not easy, but it is also not complicated. It takes time, but it is not difficult to learn. Relative to the really hard stuff we all face in life, changing a school is not hard, but it can be uncomfortable. This kind of change is relatively new to schools, but it is time-tested in almost every other institution across a wide array of sectors that have adapted to external and market changes for hundreds of years. Schools do not need to create a new pathway or set of practices; they just need to *adopt* what we know works and *adapt* those practices to the specific challenges that schools present.

In this section, we will look at what I call the Five Big Tools of Strategic School Change. For some of these, there are entire *bookshelves* and courses of study at business schools. The good news is that, like many truly elegant tools we find in life, the basics are really not that complicated. The core elements are easy to grasp, and if you just start using them, you and your team can master them relatively quickly. Think of these tools as hammers and screwdrivers, not some fancy programmable machine. Just pick up the basics and start using them; you and your school team will learn as you go.

One more note: *All of these tools work at all scales!* Don't think of them as only working at the scale of an entire school or district. They work for *any* change, down to grade levels, departments, individual classrooms, and even for individual teachers and students. I have seen first graders use elements of design-based thinking and third graders who are more than able to understand and use basic steps of organizational change! The more that school stakeholders start to feel comfortable using these tools, the faster you can say your school has shifted from being a culture based on teaching to a culture focused on learning, growing, and evolving in concert with the world around us.

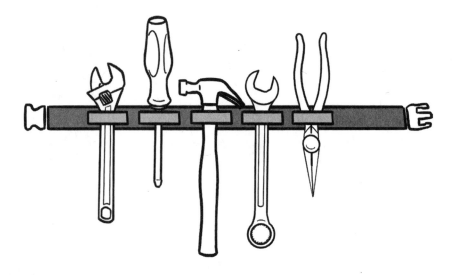

Whether they know it or not, successfully innovative schools have discovered a path that looks a great deal like that designed by organizational change guru John Kotter. It is a great structure on which to build your value-enriching change initiatives!

Big Tool # 1: Kotter(+)

Key Steps to Effectively
Changing Schools

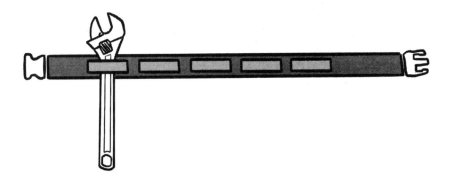

The best teachers are those who already know something that we don't understand and then have the ability to make learning it relatively easy. John Kotter is one of those best teachers. His field is the process of organizational change. I am embarrassed to admit that I had not heard of Kotter until several years ago, well after I started working with schools on helping them to engage in their respective journeys of transformation. I am an experiential learner; I learn what works and then try to create a model to help others create success. Several years ago, I realized that the steps taking place in effectively changing schools were very similar to those preached by Kotter. Convergence like this should not be a surprise; it reinforces the fact that good models actually do work.

I call this first big tool "Kotter(+)" because I have added a few tweaks and some language for educators. I strongly recommend Kotter's most famous and popular book *Our Iceberg Is Melting* (2016). It's a fable about penguins. It takes about an hour to read and covers all eight of the main steps in the model. For most school leaders, penguins and icebergs are about all the research you need in order to place this key tool on your tool belt.

With humility, and based on what I see effectively transforming schools putting into practice, I have distilled Kotter's eight steps down to six (see Figure 6.1).

Figure 6.1 Six Steps to Effectively Changing Schools

1. Build a sense of urgency around a big opportunity.
2. Unwrap and articulate a "North Star."
3. Accelerate movement by removing barriers.
4. Research, design, prototype, and test.
5. Visibly celebrate significant early wins.
6. Institutionalize changes in culture.

Six Steps to Effectively Changing Schools

1. Build a sense of urgency around a big opportunity.

Urgency can be born of passion, excitement, and potential. It can also be born of fear and uncertainty. Often, it is a combination of these that brings a community to the point where the opportunity and promise of change overcomes our individual and collective fear of the unknown. Many organizational change practitioners say that an individual or group will change once the pain of changing is less than the pain of *not* changing. In the case of our schools, the community must unwrap for themselves that the way we have "done school" for decades does not, in fact, reflect our greatest aspirations and best understanding of how great learning takes place. The community must collectively decide what future they are preparing our students for. They must decide if the need to change is truly urgent.

In virtually all of the schools I have worked, once large, diverse groups of stakeholders realize that how we "do" school today is *not* meeting their aspirations, most feel a profound sense of urgency to change. Some do not. That's OK. Getting 100 percent agreement on 100 percent of new ideas is a false hope and a bad goal. I generally suggest that when 80 percent of the community agrees with 80 percent of a set of aspirations or recognition of a problem, that is more than enough consensus to start moving. Of the remainder? The group will reach consensus on some of the rest over time. Some people will never embrace the sense of urgency. Some never want to be part of a movement. Move anyway.

2. Unwrap and articulate a "North Star."

The next step is to clearly identify the core elements of the community's aspirations for the future. In my work with schools, this is *the most critical step* in school change! Many schools have figured out that the old model of learning is not preparing our students for VUCA world and the jobs of the future. Schools that change successfully create a common aiming point rooted in their values and aspirations around great learning. I started using the term *North Star* for a good reason: The real North Star *is* an aiming point. None of us are ever going to *actually* get to the real North Star. But depending on where we are in the Northern Hemisphere, we all can share a common compass direction, even though our paths to move in that direction can and will be different. (For our friends in the Southern Hemisphere, of course, we can substitute the Southern Cross if you want to stick with celestial aiming-point metaphors.)

I will go into more detail about North Stars later in the book, but for now, suffice to say that a good North Star is a clear statement of *unambiguous, aspirational* directions that you can hand to a new teacher at your school with the advice, "Use this to guide the learning experience you will co-create with your students, and you will be contributing to the growing value of our school."

3. Accelerate movement by removing barriers.

We have all heard the complaint that changing a school or district is like turning an aircraft carrier. We have built so much inertia into our school systems that change is cumbersome, and the larger the system or part of the system we are trying to change, the more inertia we have to overcome. For megadistricts, that inertia is pretty fearsome, and I don't pretend that it is at all easy to overcome. But for most schools and districts, we have to throw out the convenient "this-is-like-turning-an-aircraft-carrier" excuse because there are wonderful examples all over the country and around the world of schools and districts with the same obstacles and inertia facing *your* school system that *have* started to make fundamental changes. (The big levers for how they are doing this is the basis for my 2017 book, *Moving the Rock.*) They do it by finding their collective North Star, then setting the real expectation that "we are going to move toward that star," and then repeatedly giving both permission and support to *just start moving.* This might involve promoting risk taking, celebrating failure, pushing authority down to the sites and classrooms, changing how decisions are made, streamlining approval procedures, and training leadership. As one principal I worked with in Santa Fe, New Mexico, put it to his staff, "Let me be really clear about this: If what you choose to do is in the best interests of our students and their learning, I am going to support you every bit of the way."

> We have to throw out the "turning-an-aircraft-carrier" excuse because there are examples all around the world of schools with the same obstacles that have started to make fundamental changes.

4. Research, design, prototype, and test.

This is where the (+) in "Kotter(+)" mostly begins. As you will see with Big Tool #2, there is tremendous overlap when you start to employ the practices of design-based thinking. Once you have a solid North Star and have cleared obstacles that impede incipient movement, the actual heavy lifting of change involves figuring out "what" the changes will be and "how" the school as an organization will get there.

There are two big keys to this step. *One size does not fit all,* and *you don't have to reinvent the wheel.* I have worked with underserved public schools and exclusive, expensive East Coast boarding schools. Some of what works for these schools is similar, and some is not. You have to design with the specific users in mind. This is the process that has come to be known as "design thinking," and there are tons of free resources and many experienced practitioners who can help train your community in how to design, learn by design, become more effective through design, and make change fun by design. The people in your school, from administrators in the central office to the students in the classroom, become *owners, not recipients* of the change. You become an organization with dozens, hundreds, or thousands of people who can lead change effectively, as opposed to one in which most of those people are waiting to be told what to do.

5. Visibly celebrate significant early wins.

Everyone loves a winner. Success breeds success. Humans gravitate toward the winning team. As schools go through a process of strategic change, they find that some proposed changes will take a long time, require multiple stakeholder agreements, and may prove risky (think major changes to all-school systems, such as schedule revisions, changes to the physical plant, shifts in all-school policies and practices on student assessment, matriculation requirements, etc.). Other changes can be implemented without much fuss; they are what I call "low-hanging fruit" (individual classroom practices, student-centered pedagogy, curriculum or lesson changes, decision-making procedures, etc.). What I have found in leading rapid prototyping sessions with teacher–admin–student design teams at dozens of schools is that *many* creative ideas fall into this category of "low-hanging fruit." They can be implemented *tomorrow* if the team just decides to do so. We need to celebrate the heck out of those early wins (and remember, a failure can still be a win) with as much support, publicity, and tangible reward as we can muster. We need to scream, "This is what winning looks like, and you can do it, too!"

> We need to celebrate the heck out of those early wins (and remember, a failure can still be a win) with as much support, publicity, and tangible reward as we can muster. We need to scream, "This is what winning looks like, and you can do it, too!"

6. Institutionalize changes in culture.

It does absolutely no good to change an organization if those changes are founded in a cult of personality, if the organization is going to backslide as soon as a superintendent, principal, school head, division leader, grade or department head, or charismatic teacher moves on. Real change requires *cultural* change. Ensuring that strategic change is a sustainable legacy and not a flash in the pan requires a long-term, *strategic-level* commitment that may exceed the tenure of a particular school leader. This is the long-term work of school change; it takes long-term vision, planning, and sustained, *systematic* execution. Perhaps most importantly, it takes leaders who can leave their ego aside and realize that they may not be around to see the final fruits of what they have planted.

That is Kotter(+). It works. In Appendix I, there are a number of activities that link to these steps. There is a lot more to learn through the experience of doing "Kotter-like" change work, but it is the first Big Tool for your school's collective tool belt!

BIG QUESTIONS FOR YOUR COMMUNITY

1. Does your school community feel an urgent need to change in some significant way? What discussions have you had that might reveal an urgent need?

2. Do you have an agreed-upon North Star vision of the future for our school? How do you know that it is actually agreed upon?

3. How can you best celebrate those who lead the way toward change, and the progress they are making, in ways that excite others to join?

The days of traditional committee-based work,
run by a titular team leader, are gone. We know
how to stimulate truly creative thinking and use
the power of empathetic user engagement to
find new, possibly even audacious solutions to
our most important problems.

Big Tool #2: Design-Based Practice

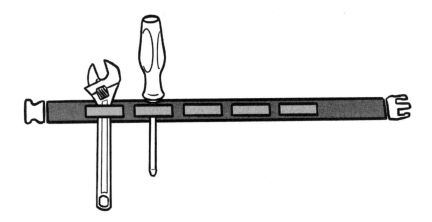

I had the distinct honor of sitting down with David Kelley at the Stanford d.school a few years ago, right after the publication of my 2014 book, *#EdJourney*. David is widely known as the godfather of design thinking. He was one of the early pioneers of Silicon Valley who realized that designing with the needs and perspectives of the user in mind could unleash value-building innovative potential. Design thinking is now a global industry and a course of learning that has positively infected almost every major college and university in the United States and around the world, and it is increasingly present as a guiding light for innovation in K–12 school systems.

In our meeting, David was so warm and friendly that I felt slightly comfortable quipping, "Isn't design thinking just great problem solving using lots of sticky notes?," to which he laughed and agreed. That is a radical oversimplification, but sticky notes certainly have become a staple of collaborative thinking among teachers and students over the last decade!

I use the term *design-based practice* as opposed to *design thinking* with purpose. The process of effectively solving a problem did not suddenly arise out of the Silicon Valley stew in the 1980s. What David and others have managed to capture within their design thinking protocols is a *set of tools*—I sometimes call them *arrows in a quiver*—that are useful at all scales and at various stages as we tackle a range of problems and opportunities we all encounter in life. I will not even try to lay out the entire design-based thinking pathway here. (There are tremendous free resources available specifically for educators; you can start with the education web pages of the Stanford d.school and the Mt. Vernon Institute for Innovation.)

There are many reasons why design-based practice works well for schools, but the most important are these:

- It helps us find the right problem to solve; it keeps us from jumping too quickly to solutions. Schools are busy, pressurized workplaces. There is an urgency to solve a problem as quickly as possible, to get it off the front burner, because another one is coming right behind it, and, by the way, we need to get back to teaching students. But creating fast solutions to the problem of the moment almost never results in the *best* solution. When I lead school teams through design challenges, whether they take place over one hour or an entire school year, *my* key challenge is often just to keep teams from jumping to what they *think* is the inevitable solution before they have let the design process work.

- Educators are here to serve, and we need to deeply know and understand who we are serving. What do they need in their lives? What do they want? What problems do they have that we can help solve because they overlap with our own vision of great learning? Empathy is at the heart of design thinking. Many educators are naturally empathetic, which is why design-based processes work so well in schools.

If you are not familiar with design thinking, here is a very brief overview of the main points, followed by a few examples of how they can be used, while expanding creativity, saving time, and strengthening user buy-in to both the process and product of strategic change. Good design-based thinking is quite different from a more traditional process in which a leader convenes a committee around a table to solve a problem. Think of a problem facing your team or your school, and imagine a process that goes through the five simple steps outlined in Figure 7.1.

Figure 7.1   Five Simple Steps of Design-Based Thinking

1. **Good design starts with radically expansive, creative, even wild imagining.** We can distill, filter, and eliminate what won't work later in the process. But if we start with a large number of (possibly wild) ideas, the odds of coming up with something innovative (value-boosting) are greatly enhanced.

2. **Design challenges start with three simple words: "How might we . . .?"** We use these words because there is no one answer to that question, and in that expansiveness lies the potential for novel solutions. At the outset, we are not looking for just one potential idea, but *many* ideas that *might* collectively lend elements to the best solution.

3. **We seek to understand the needs of the user for whom we are designing.** In schools, our users are students, teachers, administrators, hourly employees, parents, potential families, community members, colleges, employers, and more. If we don't understand *their* needs and wishes, we will fail in our design. Design thinking requires that the designers empathetically understand the needs of users and not design from just their own point of view.

4. **We create one or many rough prototypes of potential solutions**. We test these and gather feedback, and then we come up with the next iteration and the next and the next.

5. **We produce something, often sooner than it feels comfortable, and put it into practice:** a pilot program, a new course of study, classroom practice, organizational structure, a decision-making process. The mantra of design-based work, and the gasoline of the engine of much of twenty-first-century innovation, is "Fail fast and fail forward" because that is how we learn and evolve in a rapidly changing world. We learn by doing, refining, and doing again.

The design process can take a few minutes or a year. I have led hundreds of school teams through rapid design challenges that take an hour or less, and many of the resulting prototypes have been implementable as soon as the challenge was completed. Other challenges take a year, largely because of the need to truly engage users and research what is already being done at other schools or in noneducation organizations.

A good design process has two big results. The first is that it produces something that can change practice at the school in ways that will benefit users, that will *build value*. The second is that the *process itself is the product*. The process of design-based work builds both a comfort and capacity for change. It builds cultural confidence; it creates innovation DNA in the school. It turns recipients of instructions into active change agents with their own skin in the game. It is the school version of the old adage that it is better to teach a hungry person to fish than to just give him or her a fish to eat.

> A good design process has two big results: (1) It produces something that can change practice at the school in ways that will benefit users, that will *build value*. (2) The *process itself is the product*.

What Does a Good Design Process Look and Feel Like?

Great design benefits from large, diverse groups of users. Holding design events in a large room or gym with lots of wall or window space where teams can make their learning visible creates energy and a sense of "Yes, we can!" There are a lot of design-based activities in Appendix I, but Figure 7.2 has just a few shared elements that will help promote effective design-based practices.

At the point that design-based thinking becomes even *somewhat* comfortable at your school, Big Tool #2 is on your school's tool belt. In schools that adopt this method of collaborative problem solving, we see leadership teams writing sticky notes before the person with the highest title opens her or his mouth; faculty meetings that start with five minutes of empathetic data gathering around a big question of common interest; entire school communities that begin to understand that not every discussion is about coming to a decision; school teams that realize they can come up with a potential solution in 30 minutes if that is all the time they give themselves. We see the

Figure 7.2 Guidelines for Design-Based Activities

- **Use sticky notes.** People are much more likely to share ideas and insights, particularly if they might be viewed as controversial, if the sharing is anonymous. Sticky notes allow you to generate, view, sort, and synthesize huge numbers of ideas without becoming bogged down in debate and discussion.

- **The more people the better.** In good design, we can break any size group into effective working teams of five to eight people. Design works as well with a group of 200 (in fact much better) as with a group of 15.

- **The more diversity the better.** More people from as many backgrounds and perspectives as possible in the same room lead to better design. Every school team on which I have included students in the process reports it was the most powerful element of the process. The adults kick themselves for not having students authentically included in every sort of discussion from "what book should be included on the reading list" to big, strategic questions.

- **Don't do for others.** Designing is a hands-on game. Every time "leaders," usually with the best of intentions, say something like, "I can prepare that ahead of time," they have just robbed the team members of their ownership of the process.

- **"We" designed this solution.** The ideas that emerge are not handed down by a principal, department head, or superintendent. Stakeholders realize they are not making a change because "mommy or daddy told us to." They are making the change because "we," the community of stakeholders, designed it based on our values, experience, and expertise.

- **Failure is always an option.** Not all prototypes are worthy of becoming a pilot project, and not all pilots succeed. That is the way of the world—and especially of VUCA world. This is tough for school people because failure has had such a negative connotation in schools. But rapid, small failures and iteration are much better than big failures with big human and capital costs.

- **Building a shared language around innovation.** As people become more comfortable with the experience, you start to hear forward-leaning comments like, "I don't know how this fits, but let's hang on to it just in case" and "I'm not sure I see where this is going right now, but I'm willing to see more." Most powerfully, you start to hear these comments from some who started out as the least comfortable and least accepting of change, which is a huge boost to other tentative innovators on your team.

- **The next time is easier.** Most people are confused at the beginning of a design challenge: "Why can't we just solve the problem? Why are we going through all of these steps?" And then, as the prototypes are being delivered and they see ideas that never occurred to anyone at the outset when they were rushing to solve a problem that may not have been the right problem to solve, the "ah-ha" moments kick in. It is then we hear, "Now I get it" and "That wasn't so hard."

change from a school where most people are shy of trying; are worried about sharing a new idea that might be considered too radical; are waiting to be told what to do next to a school where "trying" is a badge of honor and most of the adults in the school feel that they are part of "trying."

BIG QUESTIONS FOR YOUR COMMUNITY

1. What is the level of cultural creativity at your school right now, and why do you think so?

2. When faced with a problem, does your team first question what problem they are actually trying to solve?

3. Who crafts solutions at your school—those with the loftiest title or those whose job it is to implement the solution?

4. What role do the users play in helping to design solutions that will impact them?

Educators know it as "learning by design" or
"backward design." Just as you create learning
units by first defining outcomes, we need to use
the time-tested logic model to ensure that we
design toward an aspirational future and not
get frustrated by resource limitations before we
can even start to build.

CHAPTER 6

Big Tool #3: The Time-Tested Logic Model

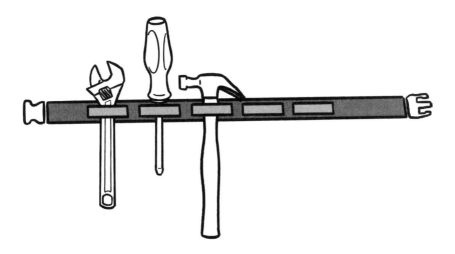

Many educators are familiar with the process of backward design or "learning by design." We know that the best way to design a learning unit is to start with the outcome you want students to achieve and then work backward to the best way to achieve those outcomes. Yet when we start discussions about making changes *beyond* the classroom, many educators abandon what they know about backward design. We immediately leap to proposing solutions and protecting or reallocating resources before we have determined the outcomes we want to achieve.

The basic concept of backward design, the logic model (see Figure 8.1), has probably been a primary tool of good problem solvers and strategists for millennia. Formal logic models have been a staple of business, science, and engineering for at least the last 50 years, and I am sure the actual practice in these fields is much older than that. We find it reflected in philosophers, writers, generals, and strategists ranging from Machiavelli to Sun Tzu to Julius Caesar.

Logic model thinking and planning works at all scales; for schools, this means it should be a principal tool for classroom teachers working out lesson plans and learning outcomes; for administrators making teams more effective and processes more efficient; and for long-range planners who need to ensure that their aspirations for the future are supported by what is *actually* taking place at the school.

Figure 8.1 Logic Model

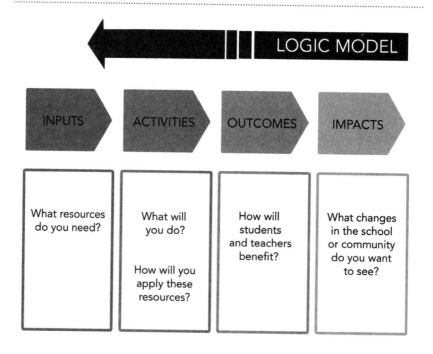

LOGIC MODEL

| INPUTS | ACTIVITIES | OUTCOMES | IMPACTS |

What resources do you need?

What will you do?

How will you apply these resources?

How will students and teachers benefit?

What changes in the school or community do you want to see?

There is tremendous overlap between the use of a logic model and good design-based thinking. In some ways, the logic model is almost the Cliffs-Notes version of a full-blown design challenge. Educators have used a version of the logic model for curriculum development for years. We have *not* tended to use it when we tackle thorny problems that might impact the whole school. As soon as the discussion elevates to these levels, school stakeholders reflexively shift into turf-protection mode. They want to make sure they are not going to lose time, students, physical spaces, FTEs, or budget. This default to the wrong end of the logic model immediately kills it off as a useful tool. Resources such as time, budget, and FTEs come at the end of the logic model, not the beginning (see Figure 8.2 for the four basic steps of a logic model translated into school language).

Perhaps the most powerful impact of the logic model is that it forces educators to *not* jump to the default solution: *time.* In virtually every school I have ever worked, as soon as we start looking at how educators would like to change, there is an almost-immediate leap to "just give me more time and we can do all of those things." But time is a resource, and resources are allocated at the *end* of the logic process, not the beginning. Rein in that urge to allocate a precious resource before you have clearly defined how you want to use it.

If I were running a school, I would hang large prints of the logic model in every office and classroom. Everyone in our school—from students to senior

Figure 8.2 The Four Basic Steps of a Logic Model

1. **Impacts**: What changes in the school or community do you want to see? Paint a picture of the best future. At an all-school or districtwide level, these impacts should reflect your community's winning aspiration. At a school or classroom level, teachers might rely on a "profile of a graduate" or simply on learning standards to create that picture of the future. An important check, however, is at this first stage: Do the impacts that each teacher might envision align to that of the entire school? Will the ideas percolating in this teacher's model support or weaken the all-school value proposition?

2. **Outcomes**: If the school, community, or world were to change as you hope, if that best future you painted in your impacts statement were to evolve, how would your students, teachers, and larger community stakeholders *benefit*? How will the humans in the equation be better off if we make those changes? If the school has clearly defined a set of impacts in its North Star or vision statements, then they de facto believe that members of the school community *will* benefit by moving closer to those results.

3. **Activities**: What will we actually *do* in order to achieve these impacts and outcomes? What will we do in the classroom? How might we make decisions in a different way? How might our subjects or curricula be reordered? How might we collaborate with colleagues in ways that support creativity? What will we choose to start doing; what will we stop doing; what will we keep doing? This is where the professional educators and students need to take the lead and decide *how* to deliver great learning as frequently and deeply as possible.

4. **Inputs**: What resources do you need for those activities to succeed? How will we reallocate resources when we start, keep, and stop various activities? How will your school decide to allocate the five precious resources that all schools have: people, time, space, money, and knowledge?

administrators and parents—would learn to think about consequences and plan backward. They would learn that resources are "fungible"; we can move at least some resources around as we choose, but if we don't agree on *why* we are allocating those resources in a particular way, then it will always just be a fight where the strongest and loudest win, which is about the surest way to kill buds of innovative change.

Ultimately, the power of the logic model is that it builds the actual implementation of alignment between what you *say* you are going to do (aspirations and promises) with what you *actually deliver* each day to your users. It also has the power of a built-in measurement tool: Are we on a path to deliver our intended outcomes or not? This is the very heart of your value proposition, and schools that continue to strengthen their value propositions will thrive more than those that do not.

BIG QUESTIONS FOR YOUR COMMUNITY

- What evidence of backward design can you identify in the learning experiences at your school?

- Describe a time when you set an aspirational goal before you thought about how to achieve that goal.

- How might your team keep from defaulting to "more time" as the solution until you have worked through the rest of the logic model?

As with the logic model, we have a time-tested
stairway upon which successfully innovating
organizations can climb. If these key elements
are in place or can be developed, there is an
excellent chance that significant, sustainable
change will occur!

Big Tool #4: The School Innovation Stairway

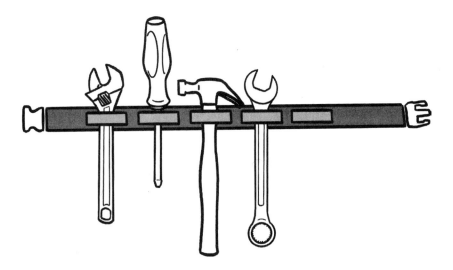

While the Kotter(+) model provides the *actions* of successful organizational change, we also need to ensure that critical *pieces* are in place for successful change to take place. We might think of these pieces as the *resources* and *nutrients* that allow change to thrive. As with a living organism, a process of strategic change will flourish if all of the nutrients are present; lack of any one critical resource can be fatal, even if the others are found in abundance. Mixing metaphors at will here, we can also think of these pieces as links in a chain or steps on a ladder: When any one fails, the chain or ladder breaks (see Figure 9.1).

Like the logic model, the stairway of successful organizational innovation has been around in some form since at least the 1980s. The earliest reference I could find to the particular stairway that I have adopted and modified is Dr. Mary Lippet in 1987 (though I cannot confirm a copyright of it). Based on my experiences working with schools and sharing processes and results with others who work with schools on change management, I think there are at least these eight critical steps in the stairway. The figure looks complicated, but it really is not. It shows that the way to *success* (top-right corner) is to have or build these pieces; missing any of the pieces leads to something short of success. In Figure 9.2, we see how these steps manifest in school terms.

The good news is that many schools already have strength in many of the areas listed in Figure 9.2! The bad news is that a school can be strong in all but one and still fail. This stairway is not a *recipe* for effective change, like Kotter(+). It is a valuable *checklist* and place to start a planning discussion. Where are we strong? Where are we deficient? How will we build on our strengths and mitigate our weaknesses?

Figure 9.1 Stairway of Successful Innovation

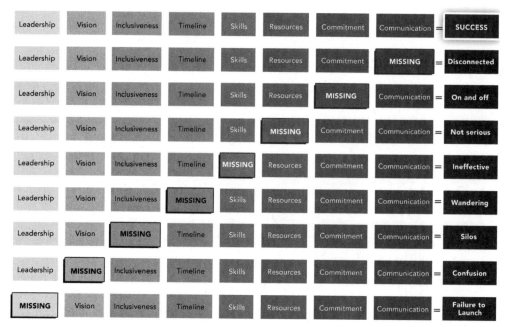

Source: Adapted from Lippet, M. (1987) and Knoster, T. (1991).

Figure 9.2 Eight Critical Steps to Successful Innovation in Schools

1. **Leadership**: While the stairway is not necessarily linear (the pieces do not have to be in place in the order from bottom to top), the one that is an *absolute prerequisite* to the others is *leadership*. Without the very visible support of titular leaders who have the authority to hire, fire, promote, and support their teams, significant change in school culture and program is extremely unlikely. But good leadership can be ephemeral. Leaders come and go, and if the value of the organization, or the strategies it is using, are vested only in a leader who leaves, then sustainable change is virtually impossible. Therefore, the "leadership" step of the stairway must be rooted in a culture and practice that will succeed the tenure of any one titular leader.

2. **Vision**: A good vision is a North Star—a set of clear, aspirational goals that differentiates your school from other schools and is clearly understood and acted on by members of your team. Vision is *not* a tagline or a few sentences full of lofty, poorly defined platitudes. Vision is *understandable* and *implementable* by those who are tasked with delivering value.

3. **Inclusiveness**: If we include large groups of user/stakeholders, they have skin in the game; if we don't, many will find reasons to *not* shift the school out of a relatively comfortable status quo. Good leaders find ways to include stakeholders in the creation and design of change-oriented projects. This does not mean that everyone becomes a decision maker. Decisions may still be made by a senior administrator or review committee or a board. But the real work of change should be open to all who want to play!

4. **Timeline**: Change cannot be open ended; we can't fall into the pit of talk, talk, talk. Good design requires us to *deliver*—and often more quickly than we have in the past. We need to set definitive goals and deadlines for when they will be met.

5. **Skills**: Just as we don't expect students to know things all on their own, we cannot expect educators to enact changes for which they are not professionally prepared. We need to provide and support our teams with the skills that are required in order to enact value-rich change.

6. **Resources:** Like most other things in life, schools need nutrients to survive and thrive. The two most important resources that positively impact change in schools are *professional development* (skill building) and the *time* needed to acquire and practice those skills.

7. **Commitment**: Nothing kills innovation faster than the idea that "this is the flavor of the month" or "just wait and the pendulum will swing back." Schools have to be *organizationally committed* to long-term strategic changes. If commitment wavers each time a new department chair, principal, or superintendent is hired, real change is doomed.

8. **Communication**: This is one of the most common weak links for schools. It does no good to design and enact change if no one knows about it. Both internal and external communications are required to design change and celebrate early wins. Communication must be frequent, on point, and well planned. If you want people to rally to your flag, your school needs to be full of good storytellers.

For many schools that are ready to use this tool, the most common strengths I see are leadership and inclusiveness. The most common deficiencies I see are in the lack of a strong North Star–type vision, the skills needed to deliver learning in a new paradigm, and a powerful and sustained communication plan. And remember, this stairway is an effective tool at the subschool level as well. If a division or department or just a group of forward-leaning teachers is ready to tackle a change, and they want that change to be successful and sustainable in the long term, this stairway is a great tool for their belt.

BIG QUESTIONS FOR YOUR COMMUNITY

1. For which steps does your school have the most current strength? How will you leverage those?

2. For which steps does your school have current weaknesses? How will you begin to mitigate those?

3. Who in your school community owns each step in the Innovation Stairway?

4. Whose input do you need to verify your strengths on the stairway? Are you including a diverse group of users in this evaluation?

Schools are a system; changing one part of the
system without understanding the ripple effects
on others is a recipe for frustration, outright
failure, or both. Working systematically is more
complicated than attempting one-off solutions . . .
but it works in the long run.

10

Big Tool #5: Understanding the School System

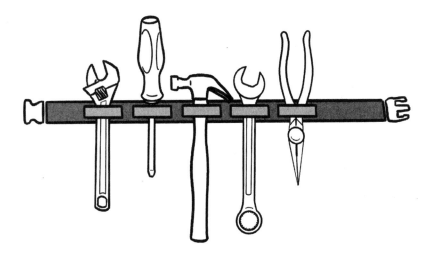

Imagine what would happen if a symphony conductor said, "I think I'll change what the clarinet section is doing in the third movement" or if the trumpet players got together at a bar one night, and one of them said to the others, "Hey, I'm getting some great feedback from my friends in the audience that we should player louder and faster." What if the quarterback on a football team decided to throw a route differently without discussing those changes with his receivers or if the manager on an auto assembly line came in one day and told her workers, "I need you to put in a new type of engine assembly, but don't slow down the line."

This doesn't happen in high-performing organizations because orchestras, athletic teams, and assembly lines are complex systems. What happens in one part directly impacts many or all of the other parts. That is what a system is: a set of interrelated parts and processes that are effective when they work together. Schools are systems, too. We know this in our gut, yet all too frequently, we forget it in practice.

In 2012, I used the term *silo* for the first time in a school workshop. I asked a group of educators what that term meant in the context of how organizations operate. Eighty percent of them returned a blank stare; to them, *silos* referred to a tall cylinder for storing grain somewhere in Nebraska.

Silos are the cells in which we each live and work, separate from others. Schools are some of the most "silo-ized" organizations on the planet. Like a set of Russian nesting dolls, *at a minimum* we have silos of classrooms, subjects, grades, divisions, and campuses—and more silos of teachers, administrators, parents, and "others." In 2018, a principal told me about a teacher who had taught for *28 years* at the same school in the same district and in that time had *never* visited another teacher's classroom during the school day. That is what silos do to us.

For decades, schools have changed when a leader or a group of teachers says something like "Let's teach a new math curriculum in the primary grades" or "Maybe we should assess students on something more authentic than tests" or "We don't have enough time in our periods each day to teach what we want." Schools and districts have tackled these problems one after the next in what an electrician would call *in series*.

> Highly functioning organizations don't tackle changes like this one at a time. They tackle them *in parallel*, as would a conductor, coach, or the manager of a good factory.

Highly functioning organizations don't tackle changes like this one at a time. They tackle them *in parallel*, as would a conductor, coach, or the manager of a good factory. Changing curriculum even in a single grade might impact instructional practices, professional growth, and the uses of both time and space, which often have ripple effects in other grade levels. Good school systems are *highly integrated:* if you push on one part, other parts have to move (see Figure 10.1). You may wish it were not so, but that is just how systems work.

Several years ago, my colleague Bo Adams imagined what he called a "pedagogical master plan." An architect, he reasoned, creates a set of

Figure 10.1 School Systems: If You Push on One Part, Other Parts Should Move

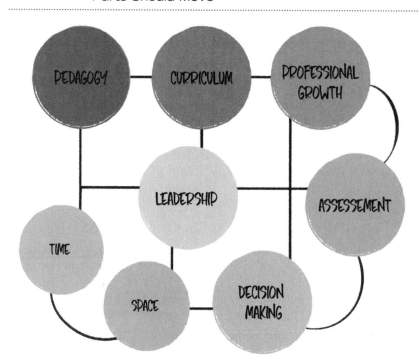

blueprints for a building, and in that set of blueprints, the architect coordinates the "system" of the building: a sheet each for plumbing, electrical, framing, foundations, roofing, and the like. All of the sheets have to work together, or the building does not perform well. You can't have a good building if the blueprint for the plumber doesn't line up with the blueprint for the framer who builds the walls or the civil engineer who places the water lines.

Why, Bo wondered, should schools not have a similar set of blueprints that comprises the main function of a school: learning. The "sheets" he recommended were these: curriculum, pedagogy, instructional practices, assessment, time, space, leadership, and professional development. He correctly argued that schools spend *vast* amounts of time and treasure developing sets of blueprints for the *buildings* on their campuses, but virtually no time creating a similar systems map for their core mission, learning.

The idea of a systems map is key to effective change. It is utterly futile to think that we can change one of the elements of Bo's set of blueprints without changing the others, just as we would not change the notes for the woodwinds or brass without modifying the parts of the other sections of the orchestra. They are intimately interconnected. If we are serious about preparing our students to become more creative, collaborative, critical thinkers, for example, the changes we have to invoke lie on every sheet of Bo's set of blueprints. Some of those changes may be minor; others will be profound.

Making changes in parallel across many elements of a system is complicated! It's a lot easier to change one bit here this year and one bit over there the next year. When we try to change too much, too fast, people feel as if they are being forced to drink from a firehose. Yet in virtually every school I have worked with, once I suggest this tool nearly everyone nods her or his head in agreement. It just makes common sense that we should not, for example, invest in a new physical space without clarity around the kind of learning that space will promote, what pedagogy we are trying to amplify, and how we are going to train teachers to be most effective there.

The key to the "drinking-from-a-firehose" problem is not to tackle too many big changes at once. It is vastly better in the long run, in terms of delivering a solid value proposition, to make a few changes deeply and thoroughly than to skip from one issue to the next without connecting the important elements of your school system.

> It is vastly better in the long run, in terms of delivering a solid value proposition, to make a few changes deeply and thoroughly than to skip from one issue to the next without connecting the important elements of your school system.

Many educators are not natural systems thinkers. That's OK; it is a learnable skill. A key element of strategic leadership and design is to understand what must be coordinated and which silos we might leave standing for another day. Bo's elements of the school operating system are a great tool to use as a checklist when we make these decisions.

BIG QUESTIONS FOR YOUR COMMUNITY

1. When trying to solve a problem or make a change at your school, does your team take into account all relevant aspects of the system? Recall an example of when your school team took into account all relevant aspects of the system when designing a solution to a problem.

2. Who is responsible for ensuring that there is coordination across silos and across these major elements of the school system? Is it a team or one person? Should that change? Why or why not?

3. What are some examples of changes your school has made in the past in which the solutions were well integrated across the entire system? What are some examples in which they were not?

Start Building

I n Section I, we created the foundation for community-wide buy-in on an aspirational value proposition that will attract and retain students, parents, and educators. In Section II, we gathered key tools that your teams can use to enact changes so you can deliver on that value proposition. In this section, you live and lead the process. This is nuts and bolts: observing, building, measuring, and iterating as your school exercises the muscles of culture that embrace *both* the needs of your users *and* the elements of a great learning experience.

Education is undergoing a profound evolution, a primary consequence of which is the challenge to continue to attract students to your school. At the core of attracting students is the absolutely critical need to *turn exciting aspirations into actual practice.*

If your school community is not excited about where you are going, it will be more difficult to attract others. If you are not delivering on your aspirations, demand will wane. Some families will come, as they always have, because it is convenient or inexpensive. But consumers increasingly want to be *excited* about their choices and their experiences. Excitement comes from meeting or exceeding users' expectations, whether those have to do with college admission, connecting a student with her or his passions, vocational training, safety and security, or empowering a young person to change the world. School will never be as exciting every day for every student as going to Disney World. But within the required parameters of a K–12 education, schools that can deliver higher levels of engagement and excitement to students and parents will build their value proposition over time.

In the Kotter(+) model of organizational change, the first step is creating a sense of urgency. In my view, this is a "prequel" step for K–12 education. For decades, we have been discussing the need to fundamentally transform our education system in order to better prepare our students for the future. The "why education must change" train left the station sometime in the 2000s. If your school community has not had that discussion, has not realized the steepness of the evolutionary curve in which we find ourselves, then, like Kotter's penguins, you better send out some scouts and seriously survey your "iceberg." There are now dozens of books, videos, TED talks, full-length movies, and exemplar schools across the country and around the world filled with colleagues who are ready to help you start this conversation.

Once a school community has found that sense of urgency, whether out of fear or enthusiastic anticipation of the future, it is time to engage, to *do*. This section introduces you to a set of ideas, tools, and rubrics that we know work but have not been used by many schools in the past. We know that real innovation comes when you explore the margins of your experience; that is where this section takes you. Some of the language and ideas may be new to you, but they are well-founded. And these margins of the traditional experience may be just how you differentiate your school from all the others.

Remember: These building skills and techniques are not only applicable to all-school or all-district strategic design. Much smaller groups—grade levels, departments, and indeed student work groups in an individual class—can use these time-tested tools to get themselves focused and moving in a common direction that is *imagined, created, and implemented by and for the team*, not imposed from someone or committee that is inevitably perceived as "the other."

You interact with your team of talented educators every day. Your day is slammed with delivering core services and putting out inevitable fires. Who has time for more? But long-term value—creating that sense of "we are irresistible"—requires a different focusing point: that we ask questions of our community in ways that many have not in the past. It's not complicated; in fact, it can be fun!

CHAPTER 11

Finding the Values of Your School Community

In the preamble to Section I, I made the case that change would be far simpler if you were acting alone, if the choices you and your school team made were not impacted by the choices of many other people. But that is not the case. You exist to serve others, and the explosion of school options in the last two decades was set off not by government policies or changes to state education codes. The match that lit this fuse was the demand by families to have choices for their children's education.

It might have been simpler to not engage deeply with your community in the past, but it was never better. Finding ways to understand what our customers want and to merge those with what we know about how great learning takes place is the most important key to schools that are both sustainable and effective.

Listen and Learn

I worked as a senior administrator for a large independent school for almost 14 years. When I arrived in the late 1990s, the school did not fill all of the available seats each year until those tense days in late August and early September when, with luck and a lot of phone calls, we usually "made the number." Several years later, after implementing some new consumer-focused, personalized marketing strategies, we had a waiting line out the door at nearly every grade level. Most school leaders would deem that a success, and in terms of raw numbers, it was; for any school, attendance is the lifeblood of budgets and funding. Yet I frequently cite that particular "success" as the most glaring failure to which I contributed during the 14 years I worked at that school.

Why? Because we spent so much time and energy telling people that we were the best school in town that we never really listened to what our potential customers valued in terms of great learning. In fact, we joked about it: "Let's not ask people what they really think; we might have to do it!"

My lesson was to trade some hubris for humility. If I had to do it again, I would have suggested a very different conversation: "We passionately seek to create the absolute best learning experience for our students. We think both you and your students will like it. In striving to do this, what advice do you have for us? Tell us how we can tailor it to help you more."

It would be simple if all families valued the same education for their children, but that just is not the case. Metaphorical families in Manhattan who believe that all paths to success flow through a select number of colleges and universities have little in common with families in the rural Midwest who hope that their kids will find some reason to stay on the farm, families in the inner city who hope their kids will come home safely each day and graduate high school, or with families in Silicon Valley who see the jobs of the future vested in the ability to write good code.

"Listening" does not equate to "doing" and certainly does not require a school to compromise on its core values. But listening lies at the core of *meeting people where they are*. There is an art to listening well; I wish someone had trained me in this art many years ago because it was not natural to me. Here are a few lessons I have learned along the way:

- You come with a background of experiences, and so do your users. No matter how good your intentions, yours are not theirs. Sometimes we can't relate to others' experiences, but *trying* to be empathetic is at the heart of real listening.

- Ask open-ended questions that can't be answered with one word. Listening is about listening deeply, not just for the first ideas that pop up.

- Use lots of sticky notes or other ways for people in groups to respond anonymously. And then allow them to "wrestle" with their collective responses. We learn more from the interactions of groups than we do from the first answers each person gives.

- Don't feel the need to debate or defend. The best response to comments from users, *especially* those that have a negative twist, is often "Thank you so much" or "Tell me more about that."

- Ask *why* to help people dig more deeply into their first responses.

Listening and learning is an ongoing process, as much in our community as it is in the classroom. There are *many frequent* opportunities to gather those small bits of data that help you to keep your value proposition on a front burner where it belongs. And after gathering those ideas, making them visible and available to the community allows stakeholders to feel that they have real skin in the game, that the school has listened to what they think.

What Is Your School's Net Promoter Score?

Remember that *value* is defined as the difference between what you *say* your school will deliver and what you *actually* deliver, *as viewed by your customers*. As the diversity of learning options for families continues to explode, fewer families choose to go to their neighborhood school just because it is close to home. One of, if not *the,* most important drivers of school selection is word of mouth. When families have a choice, what they hear from friends, family, and "on the soccer field" is much more important in terms of selecting a school than any other form of advertising. That is why school organizations and leaders should be familiar with the Net Promoter Score (NPS).

Used by a wide range of industries, the NPS uses *a single question* that has proven to frequently indicate customer loyalty. If word-of-mouth recommendations are a major reason that families choose your school, then NPS is *the* key to attracting and retaining students.

Figure 11.1 tells you all you need to know: the single NPS question and how to measure the response.

Here is the big deal about NPS: According to massive studies using this tool, *only 9s and 10s are real promoters of your school.* Anyone who does *not* self-identify as a *9* or *10* on this scale is *not* going to positively impact that buzz around the neighborhood, at church, or on the proverbial soccer field.

You already know it's *not* good if your customers are frequently calling the principal in anger. But it is also *not good enough* that they are *not* calling the principal in anger.

Truly good, positive recommendations only come from people who self-identify as a *9* or a *10*. They are your only real champions. This may sound harsh, but NPS has proven true for many years and across many different sectors.

Figure 11.1   Net Promoter Score

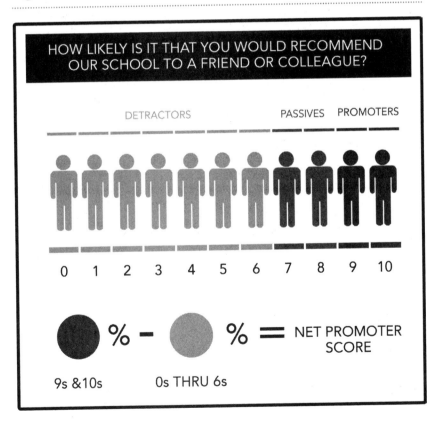

There are all kinds of resources on the Internet about NPS; just search it. While I cannot find specific data for schools, in general any NPS that is greater than zero is considered "good," while an NPS anywhere close to 50 percent is considered "great." And remember that you have to include the "passives" in the denominator when calculating percentages.

If you have reason to believe that word of mouth can positively or negatively impact what your community thinks about your school, you simply have to increase the number of people who respond as a *9* or *10* to this question. They are true champions of your school who are consistently shouting positive things about you. The best way to increase your *9s* and *10s* is to consistently know, attend to, and perform on your core value proposition and to include more stakeholders in the process of designing, delivering, and communicating about your school. When you know what the *9s* and *10s* love about your school, you can strategically and consistently deliver on those.

One Big Thing

Even with proven tools like the NPS, there is always a danger in using data to drive our decisions: We tend to follow the majority and overlook outliers. We always need to be on the lookout for that One Big Thing that might not be obvious but may have disproportionate influence. Very small things can sometimes have enormous impacts: a few parts per billion of lead in drinking water is toxic. On the other hand, a Rosa Parks or Malala Yousafzi can drive change in positive ways that have avoided thousands or millions of attempts before them.

Is there something small lurking at your school that, if it were to change, might be a key to more community support and higher, ongoing enrollment? As I cited in *Moving the Rock* (Lichtman, 2017), David Miyashiro, superintendent of Cajon Valley Schools just east of San Diego, recognized that he had an elementary school with dropping enrollment in an underserved neighborhood that did not need to lose yet another valuable local resource. His team uncovered an unexpected opportunity. A significant group of parents who had district choice options had deselected that elementary school because the school had cut back on early drop-off and late pickup options the previous year. In this working-class neighborhood of parents who often commute 45 minutes or more to work, the loss of after-hours supervision was a deal killer; they selected other schools. The impacted school refound the resources they needed to bring back before-and-after school services, and the following year, enrollment increased by 70 students.

You will almost never find that One Big Thing using SurveyMonkey. You have to get personal with people and drill down on what *they* want or need. They have to trust that you are really listening and that, even if the change that *they* want does not make the top of the list, the school is listening and responding to what is important to their users.

> You will almost never find that One Big Thing using SurveyMonkey. You have to get personal with people and drill down on what *they* want or need.

What Do Your Stakeholders Actually Value?

It's one thing to talk about value in the abstract and quite another to actually find the building blocks that will consistently deliver on that value for your school. As with much of what schools are finding in this new competitive environment, we don't have to reinvent the wheel. Other industries have been competing for centuries, and many of the lessons they have learned are transferable to schools.

People choose things that make them feel better, that maybe even make their lives better. Bain and Company's customer and marketing strategy team identified 30 ways that people perceive their lives are improved by selecting a product or service (Almquist, Senior, & Bloch, 2016). These thirty "elements of value" are arranged in four groups: Functional, Emotional, Life-Changing, and Social Impact (see Figure 11.2). These groups form a pyramid that looks a lot like Abraham Maslow's "hierarchy of human needs," first published in 1943, in which Maslow argues that all human actions are driven by needs ranging from the very basic (food, rest, reproduction) to the very lofty (moral purpose, selflessness).

Each value element has the potential to attract customers. Those at the bottom are easier to replicate by competing organizations, and those at the top tend to impassion customers the most. Companies like Apple, Tesla,

Figure 11.2 Bain and Company's Elements of Value

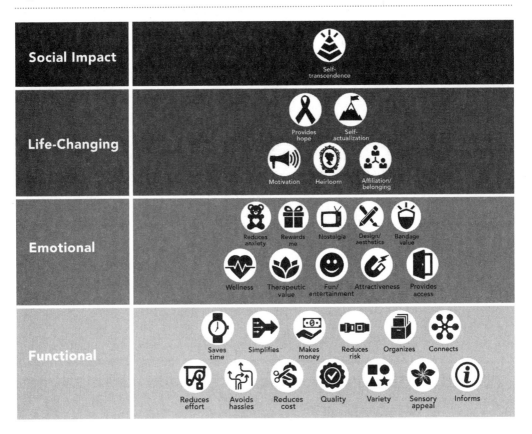

North Face, Nike, Lululemon, and Starbucks rocketed to the top of their respective industries not because their products necessarily perform better than the competition. Their products make large groups of customers *feel* better *with* the product than *without* them. The same can be said for many of the schools that are disrupting education. They have not all grown in demand because of rising test scores or a larger variety of courses. Many of them are in demand because they have found ways to deliver on the upper tiers of the value pyramid. Schools are, in fact, rich opportunities for many of the elements higher on the pyramid. Education has always held the potential to be life-changing and to provide powerful social and emotional impacts for both individuals and families.

While it is unlikely that any teacher, school, or district will find a "secret sauce" of learning that is equivalent to the first iPhone, every item on the list holds the potential for increasing a school's value proposition. While the most value-rich elements tend to lie toward the top of the pyramid, don't overlook the rest. *Innovative combinations of these elements can create and build substantial value* for individual organizations.

It is very easy for your school team to look at these thirty value generators, pat themselves on the back, and say, "Yep, we do that!" But finding examples of value is not the same as *systematically embedding those elements into the school operating system*. This is where customer feedback is critical. If you want your value proposition to include wellness, reduced anxiety, fun, hope, motivation, connections, or anything else on this pyramid, then you should hear these elements loudly and frequently from your most supportive customers when you drill down on your Net Promoter Score survey. These elements should be experienced by *many* of your community stakeholders, not just some. If not, then you have a misalignment between "promise" and "deliver," in which case you need new and more powerful strategies to deliver your value proposition.

BIG QUESTIONS FOR YOUR COMMUNITY

1. Do you know your school's Net Promoter Score? If not, how might you gather that simple information from your users? If yes, how do you use it?

2. How do your communication systems/protocols make your users feel about your school?

3. What are your parents talking about in the parking lot? What are your students saying on ratemyteachers.com?

4. Which elements of the value pyramid might excite your students, parents, teachers, and other users?

5. If you could change one thing at your school that would make it more irresistible to more people, what would it be?

At the end of the day, families expect schools to do a job. We know what some of that job is: educate our kids in foundational knowledge that they will need in order to effectively participate in a modern human society. But that is not the end of the story, and the targets and expectations are probably moving faster than we think.

CHAPTER 12

Do You Know the Jobs Your School Is Hired to Do?

In 2007, Harvard professor and innovation thought leader Clayton Christensen reoriented our thinking about how organizations can best meet their customers' needs and, in doing so, grow their business (Christensen, Anthony, Berstell, & Nitterhouse, 2007). "Most companies segment their markets by customer demographics or product characteristics and differentiate their offerings by adding features and functions," wrote Christensen. "But the customer has a different view of the marketplace. He simply has a job to be done and is seeking to 'hire' the best product or service to do it."

The Jobs to Be Done (JTBD) approach to strategic innovation has grown into a powerful way to understand the relationships between producers and consumers. How is the model most relevant to departments, schools, and districts that want to ensure ongoing or growing demand from consumers?

Seth Godin quotes Theodore Levitt of Harvard: "People don't want to buy a quarter-inch drill bit. They want a quarter-inch hole" (Godin, 2018). His point was that there are actually many ways to create a hole; one of them is by drilling it with the power drill on your workbench. But innovators are always trying to find a better way to do that job, and when they do, they put the old solution out of business. Schools are no longer immune from innovation that can put them out of business.

Godin pushes that thinking further. "No one wants a hole," writes Godin in *This Is Marketing* (2018). "What people want is the shelf that will go on the wall once they drill the hole. Actually, what they want is how they'll feel once they see how uncluttered everything is, when they put their stuff on the shelf that went on the wall. . . . They also want the satisfaction of knowing they did it themselves. Or perhaps the increase in status they'll get when their spouse admires the work. Or the peace of mind that comes from knowing that the bedroom isn't a mess, and that it feels safe and clean. People don't want to buy a quarter-inch drill bit. They want to feel safe and respected."

Stew on that for a minute. People don't want to buy a drill bit; they want to feel safe and respected. What opportunities does that kind of radically different perspective provide for a school that may see enrollment challenges today or on the horizon?

Some of the reasons parents send their children to school have remained static for decades. A big reason is that it is the law. Most parents also believe that education is on the critical path to a better life for their children. And many families don't want kids hanging around the house or getting into trouble during the day when parents are at work. For many families and for many years, the "jobs" of school have been perceived as things such as these:

- Teach children how to read, write, do math, and solve problems.

- Teach students how to interact with others.

- Prepare students for the next grade and then for college or work after high school.

- Prepare students to do well on standardized exams.

- Keep students and teachers safe within quiet, well-managed classrooms.

When we apply JTBD thinking, we find that the "jobs" that motivate parents, students, and even teachers may be evolving. Yes, parents and students still want those basics they have always wanted, but now we see answers such as the following:

- Help my child overcome obstacles.

- Help my child be future ready.

- Help my child to fulfill his or her potential.

- Help my child to become more globally aware.

- Give my child opportunities to impact the world in a positive way.

- Motivate my child to find and pursue her or his passions.

- Teach my child how to effectively work as a member of a team.

- Help my child connect with others, make friends, and find role models.

- Keep my child safe.

The more your school is competing for students, the more surgically you will have to decide just what jobs you are being hired to do and how to do those jobs exceptionally well.

Most of us would like to include *all of both lists* as JTBD. It is easier to *include* than *exclude* items on a list of what we value. But the reality is that *no school can be great at everything*. Those that try to do everything well almost always do everything "somewhere in the middle"—they don't stick out as being the "best" at anything. In other words, they don't exhibit differentiated value. The more your school is competing for students, the more surgically you will have to decide just what jobs you are being hired to do and how to do those jobs exceptionally well.

Can schools actually *choose* a path of differentiated value while *still* meeting learning standards, accommodating students with special needs, living within tight budgets, and all of the other pressures we heap on them?

Some can and are. Harrisburg School District in South Dakota believes it is being hired to treat each student as an individual, and its personalized learning track for elementary and middle school students has rapidly become more popular than the traditional learning track. IowaBIG school in Cedar Rapids believes it is being hired to give high school students a four-year, real-world learning experience with community partners to help them select college and work-ready pathways after they graduate, and demand for the school continues to increase every year. Mt. Vernon Presbyterian School in Atlanta believes it is hired to prepare students to make an impact on the world around them, and its iDiploma students are embedded with a wide range of corporate, government, and community partners to create, design, and implement impactful products and services. Design 39 Campus in Poway, California, believes it is hired to prepare students as life-ready thought leaders capable of elevating humanity. These schools, and the hundreds of others I could list and many more that I don't know about, realize that they are being hired to provide an excellent basic education in math, literacy, science, the arts, *and* something else that we as educators, parents, and students know we want from our schools.

Linking JTBD to Value and Innovation

The goal of innovation is to grow the value of the organization. JTBD creates a system by which we can better judge *which* innovations will actually result in more positive value as seen by the customers. Anthony Ulwick (2016) identifies a simple initial segmentation of jobs that we can easily identify:

1. **Functional job aspects** are the practical requirements that customers have that drive them to purchase goods and services. We might think of these as the "nuts and bolts." For schools, these would include a safe environment, teachers who know their subject and can instruct and assess students fairly, sufficient supplies and materials, a diverse set of course options, a clean campus that is accessible to families, and a standards-based curriculum that can receive accreditation and recognition for post-graduate opportunities.

2. **Emotional job aspects** are more "subjective customer requirements related to feelings and perception." They include many of the words and phrases that I and others have gathered when we ask parents, students, and teachers what they value most in a learning experience: joy, engagement, curiosity, support, rigor, collaboration, passion, community, excitement, and relationships.

Even this simple two-part system is highly relevant to schools that are seeking to build value over time. Most schools, particularly until the 2000s, focused almost exclusively on their *functional* job aspects. The entire No Child Left Behind and Race to the Top eras were focused on "doing the functions" of school better. The rise of charter schools, which has been by far the most disruptive innovation in the education marketplace in the last half century, was not solely due to customer dissatisfaction with how schools were delivering their *functional* jobs. The explosion of school choice, of which charters are one element, is due to the gap between what schools delivered and the *emotional* job aspects that parents, students, and even teachers actually want.

Ulwick's work with dozens of organizations in many industries across more than 25 years demonstrates that "if your industry is mainly focused on the *functional* aspect of the JTBD, then differentiate yourself with the *emotional* aspect." This goes straight to the heart of school transformation from a static, highly functional, one-size-fits-all "industrial age" learning model based on standardization, teacher centrism, and outdated syllabi to a "deeper learning" model that emphasizes introspection, questioning, student choice, fluidity, and personalized learning. Deeper learning provides the *functional* elements of a traditional education (students learn content), while *also* delivering those *emotional* elements that customers value at least as much, if not more.

Understanding JTBD leads to innovations that differentiate value as opposed to those that might be "great ideas" but do not excite your customers enough to turn them into true champions of your school, those *9s* and *10s* on the Net Promoter Score. Innovation is about matching customers' desired outcomes with strategies and tactics that *actually deliver* on the "job" you are hired to do.

But we know that schools are not homogenous; not all customers want their school to do the same "job" for their children. How do we decide which of the many JTBD we will actually focus on? Think about these very different JTBD by schools:

1. Keep students safe during the time they are at school.

2. Prepare students to learn in real-world settings.

Many school teams would include both of these—and many, many more—on their list of JTBD. But using this vastly simplified example of just two JTBD, how might two different schools include both JTBD in very different value propositions?

The first school's North Star elevator pitch might include, "Of course we are going to teach your students what they need to succeed in college and the workplace, but what you really need to know is that we have a uniquely powerful, laser focus on keeping your children safe during the school day."

The second school's North Star elevator pitch might be, "Of course student safety is always at the front of our minds, but we believe that students must frequently get off campus to know how to learn and live in the real world."

Two families, both of whom value academic success and who love their children, might have very different views of these two value propositions. From all of the choices they have for their kids, these two will stand out as different from the larger group of schools that simply offer the convenience of proximity to the home.

BIG QUESTIONS FOR YOUR COMMUNITY

1. Do you know the jobs that your school is being hired to do by your current and prospective families?

2. If not, how will you gather that knowledge?

3. If so, what are they, and how do you know?

4. How will your community come together in agreement on the most important and value-rich JTBD?

In a time of increasing volatility and uncertainty, effective organizations realize that leadership is not about "the general" telling everyone what to do every day, in every situation. In order to use the tools we have discussed, in order to build a value proposition that will excite current and future families, effective school leaders think and lead more like architects than like generals and dictatorial CEOs in the past.

CHAPTER 13

Lead Like an Architect

Several years ago, a team of researchers in the United Kingdom studied schools that were struggling with various change opportunities and obstacles (Hill, Mellon, Laker, & Goddard, 2016). They looked at how school leaders were attempting to meet these challenges, which leadership styles were successful and which were not. They identified five school-specific leadership archetypes, four of which proved ineffective at leading their schools through major changes and one that was highly successful. First, the *unsuccessful* archetypes—you probably know at least one school leader who fits within each of these groups!

- **The Surgeon Leader**: Like a good trauma specialist in a triage room, this type of leader identifies the single most pressing problem, rallies the team to fix it, and then moves on to the next one.

- **The Soldier Leader**: Like a great infantry officer, this leader points to the challenges ahead and rallies the team to work hard, work together, and conquer the problem in front of them.

- **The Accountant Leader**: Like a great businessperson, this leader believes that the answer to all problems lies in studying and understanding the data.

- **The Philosopher Leader**: Beloved by the faculty, this leader believes that the solution to all problems in a school is great teaching, failing to recognize that many modern schools are complex organizations with systemic issues beyond the individual classroom.

The one type of school leader that was *most* successful when faced with big, hairy challenges was the **Architect Leader**. This should not have been a surprise, as there is tremendous overlap between how architects view their work and the five tools of strategic, value-building change we addressed in the last section.

If you have ever worked with a good architect (and I have had that privilege in building both a home and school campuses), you know how an architect uses a design-based approach to first imagine and then craft the right building. It usually starts with a site visit with the clients to empathetically understand their needs. The architect asks a lot of questions, provoking the clients to dig deeply beyond *what* they want to build into *why* they want a new building and *how* they will use the building.

That first meeting might end with a really rough pencil sketch. It's the architect's way of capturing the most important elements of the clients' aspirations without getting bogged down in details. If pressed to be honest, any good architect will admit that this first sketch is probably way beyond the clients' budget; at this point, it is a piece of art that merges the clients' dream with the architect's eye and experience.

Over time, working with the client-users, a good architect redraws that first sketch many times, thinking about different floor plans, materials, building techniques, and schedules. They often tear up those first sketches completely and come up with several completely different alternative approaches. Finally, they arrive together at a solution that meets the users' needs and is affordable. In the same way, there are some very specific ways that educators, from the classroom to the boardroom, can "lead like an architect" (see Figure 13.1).

Figure 13.1   Tips on How to Lead Like an Architect

- **Observe and listen**: Schools, like buildings, are made to be used by human beings. Schools have unique qualities that fit the site, the families in the neighborhood, the community, and the learning needs of a particular group of users. My house should *not* look and function like all other houses because it serves what my family finds most valuable to us. A good architect-leader listens to the users about their unique desires, needs, and constraints before devising a solution. A good school leader does the same with her or his community of current and prospective stakeholders. Together, they co-create a learning experience that works best for *their* students.

- **Create a vision for the future that meets the needs of the user**: If we could all sketch a beautiful building, we would have less need for architects. Many school stakeholders know what they want, but they are not trained at seeing how to bring about that result. Effective school leaders help their teams gather, synthesize, and translate what they hear from users and, using those inputs, develop an aspirational vision of what the future will look like with this transformed school in the world.

- **Work from a large pallet of options, not one cookbook recipe**: Great architects can design buildings in wood, steel, stone, concrete, and more. They draw on many aesthetics and styles, not just one. Effective school leaders draw on many sources of potential solutions; they don't look for the one-stop solution that worked for one other school because the best solutions for *your* school and *your* community may be inspired by a mixture of other successes.

- **Build for the long term**: Buildings (hopefully) outlive the architect. Unfortunately, in today's school systems, leadership tenures tend to be very short. A good leader has the humility to build a success for which he probably cannot take credit over time. Effective architect-leaders ensure that their community takes into account both the short-term goals of this generation of students and the longer-horizon challenges that will face those yet to attend.

- **Seek solutions that work for diverse groups**: An effective building is designed to work well for the plumber, electrician, roofer, and many more. An effective school is like an effective building. A school architect-leader makes sure that the solution works for teachers, students, parents, lawmakers, and other community stakeholders. This does not mean that everyone in all of these groups will fall in love with 100 percent of the solution, but the architect-leaders do their best to accommodate critical recommendations. They also make sure that as many decisions as possible are left up to those who actually live with the results: the teachers and students.

- **Don't fall in love with the first draft**: This is by far the most important characteristic of the architect-leader. The first sketch of a new building is *never* right. It is a sketch in theory, often in La-La Land . . . but it is the critical first step around which all of the next steps can nucleate. The first set of detailed plans your architect delivers will always be over budget and require value engineering: choices we are forced to make to match our resources with the results we want to see. The team works on a next iteration that highlights the most value-rich elements that simply must be retained and makes choices to trim the rest. A good leader is willing to make changes after a first iteration, *even when those changes run contrary to his or her initial ideas.*

Most school leaders are not natural architect-leaders. Most school leaders with titles "above" that of department head have very similar résumés. They went to a postsecondary school of education; spent years in the classroom, most often in the humanities; took on a leadership role (department chair, grade-level leader, assistant division leader); worked as a site leader (principal, assistant head of school); and ultimately became principal of a larger or more prestigious school or worked in the district office. Because of this path, they have learned to solve problems through the lens of an educator, not an architect.

> A good leader is willing to make changes after a first iteration, *even when those changes run contrary to his or her initial ideas.*

The overlap between architect-leading and design-based thinking is powerful and pervasive; good architect-leaders find natural comfort with the big tools of strategic change. In their book, *Design Thinking for School Leaders*, veteran teacher-leaders Alyssa Gallagher and Kami Thordarson (2018) show how school leaders can shift from being "accidental leaders" to "design inspired leaders." They urge educators to become an "experience architect who designs and curates learning experiences" rather than someone who follows outdated guidebooks.

Or Lead Like a General

Architects and educators are not the only professions in which this kind of leadership paradigm is rewarded. Retired General Stanley McChrystal led American forces in Iraq during some of the most violent phases of the post-Saddam years, when Al Qaeda and affiliated groups tore the country apart in an endless series of sectarian attacks that killed tens of thousands of innocent civilians. In *Team of Teams*, McChrystal openly reflects on how the powerful, resource-rich, highly structured American forces were constantly surprised by the ragtag, loosely networked improvisation of the insurgents (McChrystal, 2015).

McChrystal and his staff had to completely rethink how large organizations are structured and managed and then rebuild everything they did in order to deal with a threat and an enemy that was vastly more dynamic and nimble. They first created strong teams that reflected much of the "architect-leader" approach: busting silos, radical transparency and sharing of ideas, distributed decision making, borrowing from other kinds of organizations, and a deep willingness to iterate based on new experiences. Then they scaled up: They rebuilt the entire command into a "team of teams," which completely disrupted the traditional, highly hierarchical organization chart with which we are all so comfortable (see Figure 13.2).

Figure 13.2 From Command to Team of Teams

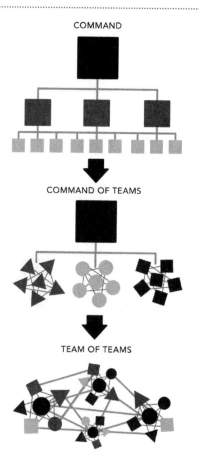

This structure allows organizations to become flexible and nimble where they have been slow and rigid in the past. It is messier, but that messiness allows both individuals and groups to respond to new challenges rather than be overrun by them. We can think of this as an organizational structure that allows many, if not all, members to lead more like architects and teams of architects. There are several keys to making this structure work:

- Leaders allow (perhaps even require) others to make decisions. They put people in place who they trust and then trust them to do the right thing.

- Individuals have access to people on other teams; the more they see and work with others, the more they trust and support each other.

- Every individual does not have a relationship with every other individual, but everyone should know someone on other teams.

- Leaders provide information so subordinates are armed with context and can take the initiative to make decisions. Everyone in the organization understands the interaction of the moving parts.

The great news is that many educators have real strengths in the design-based skills of listening, empathy, creativity, collaboration, and communication, all of which are rewarded in this more dynamic leadership structure. These strengths are not found just in the principal's office; they are pervasive among even young, inexperienced classroom teachers. It is easy for educators to lead like an architect or an effective general if we give them the opportunity and expectation to frequently practice as one.

BIG QUESTIONS FOR YOUR COMMUNITY

1. What kind of leader are you? What kind of leaders do you have on your team?

2. How might you work with your team to create a vision for the future that is highly focused on the needs and desires of your users?

3. How can you broaden the palette of options that you and your team consider when starting to design solutions?

4. What are some signs that leaders in your school are allowing others to influence their own first instincts when it comes to creating solutions?

If you lead your team as a collaborative partner, they will feel empowered to help design, and then deliver, a consistent set of services that align with the collective aspirations of your community. When teams have allegiance to a shared ideal, they are much more likely to produce that ideal at a high level than if they have an allegiance to a paycheck or a boss.

CHAPTER 14

Finding Your School's North Star

Finding and clearly articulating your school's North Star is *the most impactful step of sustainable, value-rich change.* It pulls large, diverse groups of people into ownership of strategic design. It gets many people invested with a personal stake in seeing strategy evolve and succeed. It dissolves the screen of secrecy around strategy. It produces that critical common aiming point—not a point upon which 100 percent of the community agrees 100 percent, but around which there is strong enough consent and passion to sustain the sense of urgency that drives real change and allows your school to deliver on your collective value proposition.

The process of developing a good all-school or districtwide North Star can take a few months; for a department or grade level with fewer stakeholders, it might take a few hours. Regardless of the net time spent, it is time *well spent*, as the skills that any team builds in developing this North Star for themselves are what get them personally invested when it comes to actually *making* changes in practice that might feel uncomfortable or even scary.

An effective North Star is a product of creative, collaborative, empathy-rich work, as shown in Figure 14.1.

Figure 14.1 Signs of an Effective North Star

- **It is aspirational.** Schools need to attract adults and students who want a reason to rally to *your* flag when there are so many others vying for their attention and support. There is a reason that people flock to brands like Amazon, Nike, Apple, and Tesla; they inspire us (even as they sometimes frustrate us as well). You need customers to fall in love with your school's aspirations for the future.

- **It is different.** This is the hardest part. Schools have been largely *undifferentiated* for decades. Now they are under pressure to provide a differentiated value proposition that will attract users. There may well not be enough unique value propositions to go around. Some schools will need to have highly differentiated programs in order to attract students; others are in less competitive markets and will be able to survive and thrive with a greater degree of "sameness."

- **It is a balance.** A good North Star will give teachers and administrators enough guidance to align their practice to all-school strategy while leaving them enough room to creatively design their own practice as an educator.

- **It is a point of common allegiance and "judgement."** Once the North Star is adopted, everyone in the school has a point of unity. Their affinity is no longer to "middle school" or "the math department"—they are not protectors of turf. Their allegiance is to the aspirations of the North Star. When potentially innovative ideas arise, those ideas are judged based on a very simple rubric: Does it get us closer to the North Star or not?

What follows are the steps for creating a great North Star. In Appendix I, I include a more detailed outline of how to facilitate each step in ways that will include and empower your school members.

Unwrap

First, throw out every possible boundary that fetters creative thinking: obstacles, fears, traditions, inertia, budgets, and the like. Creative design demands that we start with the fewest constraints possible. We can always filter and reduce our aspirations if we start out as big and wide as possible; the opposite is nearly impossible. The process commonly is described as looking something like the image in Figure 14.2; we start at the "wide and wild" end of the funnel.

That being said, every school has some limiting conditions that must bind their thinking, which is why I call these "boundary conditions" or "fence lines." The fewer the better, but some are real, unavoidable, and perhaps even beneficial. Boundary conditions might be things like the following:

- The physical location of the school is not going to change.
- The school will continue to meet all applicable state, federal, and local standards.
- The school will be a community that values diversity in all of its programs, hiring, and practices.
- The district is a union district and will continue to cooperate with the unions.

Within these broad boundary conditions, the community is as joyously aspirational as possible. Bring big, diverse groups of stakeholders together in one room. Leave your silos and "hats" at the door. Enter and connect with each other as "co-imaginers," not as teachers, administrators, parents, and students. The more the better; the energy of 200 people in a room is a visible and powerful stimulant to creativity in ways that cannot be replicated by a select committee of 20.

Figure 14.2 Creative Design Process

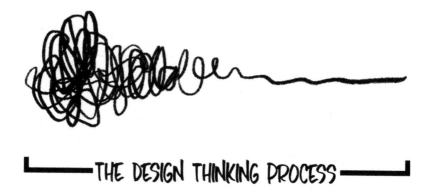

THE DESIGN THINKING PROCESS

Ask open-ended questions that allow the group to express the best version of themselves and their school at a point in the future. Allow them to dream, unconstrained by anything other than the boundary conditions. Find what is powerful and passionate in your community, even if those lie outside the lines of your current conception of "school." This is *the key* to the whole process of strategic change: If we ask the right questions, we have a good chance of coming up with the right answers!

Listen

Schools have many users: students, teachers, parents, community stakeholders, site and district administrators, college admissions offices, potential employers, the owner of the coffee shop on Main Street, the city librarian, and more. Before you start crafting your North Star, gather as much knowledge as possible from as many people as possible. Before you start *telling* your community what lies at the core of your aspirational vision, *listen* to what *they* think.

> Before you start *telling* your community what lies at the core of your aspirational vision, *listen* to what *they* think.

One of my real moments of epiphany came several years ago as a new public school, Design 39 Campus, was preparing to open in Poway Unified, just north of San Diego. D39C is not a charter school; it is a choice school. Families can enter a lottery for spots in the school, or they can send their child to the regular neighborhood school. In order to help families decide if D39C might be the right choice for them, the founding team held open meetings for prospective parents, gathering their responses to big questions, such as "What do great learning and great teaching look like to you?" Then, *after* the parents had a chance to voice their own ideas, the team said, "Thanks; now let us tell you what we are designing. We want to use what we are hearing from our community to refine our own general ideas and create a school that is different from your other options. If you fall in love with what you hear as much as we have, then this might be a great school for your child."

Marketing guru Seth Godin (2018) says that this deep, authentic connection to our community is *the key* to long-term success. "Find a corner of the market that can't wait for your attention," says Godin. "Go to their extremes. Find a position on the map where you, and you alone, are the perfect answer. Overwhelm this group's wants and dreams and desires with your care, your attention, and your focus." We can only achieve this sweet spot if we stop telling people why our school is great and listen to what they want and need.

Filter

What do you do with hundreds or thousands of pieces of information that you gather when you listen well? Who has time to make sense of it all? Isn't this why SurveyMonkey questions with pull-down menus and "on a scale of 1 to 5" are really great?

When I was in fifth grade, my mother volunteered to conduct a wide-ranging survey of parents and teachers for our local school district. They collected hundreds of paper survey forms; our job was to read them all, tally the answers, and make sense of the open-ended ones. Forty years later at my former school, we hired a graduate student to do the same thing: wade through all of those written answers and make sense of them. The answers ranged from the short and poignant to long-winded rants about why "Mr. Jones is the lousiest teacher ever!"

Hiring a consultant or finding a volunteer is the *worst* way to reduce a large data set. As with the teacher who lectures her students about the causes of the Civil War or teaches them a trick shortcut to solve a math problem, it robs the learner of the opportunity to *learn by doing*. So how do you efficiently distill a couple of hundred or a thousand sticky notes down to a useful data set? Simple: "We" do the work.

Teams read and sort what has been gathered. Not every person or every team has to read every bit. They find and share the big themes. Five teams of five people can read, organize, and share key findings from 500 sticky notes in an hour. Is every comment given equal weight? No; that is not the goal. Your goal is to let the law of large numbers work for you, to find the centers of gravity in what your community believes.

Narrow

The cream quickly rises; you will see the big themes that inspire and motivate your users. Suddenly, you have a new and clear set of guideposts. What will you do with them? Can your school be all of these things? What if they conflict?

Using the big themes as a set of guides, define your school's "best self." Describe the nonnegotiables that would make your future school the very best school for the community you serve.

The tendency, and a critical pitfall, is to turn the entire rich, savory stew of aspirations into a new "strategic plan," to celebrate the inclusive, generative process and shout *YES* to all of the wonderful goals and dreams that so deeply reflect your collective views of the perfect school. After all, if the ideas are great and they came from "us" and they align with what we know about how students learn best, why should we not strive to include *all* of them in our future work?

It is at this point that the big tools of real strategy emerge. It is at this point, when most schools begin to create long lists of tactical steps with hopeful timelines and vaguely defined metrics, that you simply *must* take a different, less comfortable path. We have created those long lists in the past because they ensure that everyone, every silo of self-interest across the department or school or district, can point to at least *something* in the plan that speaks to that self-interest. Like Congress passing a pork-loaded budget, all of the school silos can claim victory. The result is a set of guideposts with no compass heading, a plan with no strategy, a vision with so many value propositions that, as we say, it would challenge "God on a good day" to fulfill.

When diverse groups of school stakeholders take off their self-interest hats, when we force ourselves to prioritize, to make choices because we simply *can't* be all things to all people, a relatively few powerful kernels make it through the thresher. These become the nucleating elements of the North Star. The remaining products of this generative, creative process are not useless chaff! They are not discarded! In fact, many will form the basis of a growing stockpile of energy and nutrients for the innovation to come. But now the organization has a manageable set of ideals toward which they can mutually reinforce their practice, and those ideals are rich in potential future value.

> When diverse groups of school stakeholders take off their self-interest hats, when we force ourselves to prioritize, to make choices because we simply *can't* be all things to all people, a relatively few powerful kernels make it through the thresher. These become the nucleating elements of the North Star.

Write

Finally, whether the process has taken hours or months, the North Star must be written down. The community needs an artifact of their distilled aspirations, with enough detail that the value deliverers (the teachers and administrators) know how to align their compasses. People in schools change all the time; we need something that does *not* shift with every loud voice or new person in the room. *It is time to craft your actual North Star.*

If the writing is lazy, if it is full of ambiguous platitudes, then everyone can point to the result and feel that it means exactly whatever they want it to mean. If the writing is clear and unambiguous, everyone will understand the direction the North Star is leading them.

If your North Star merely defends what your school is already doing, you are telling the world that this is as good as it will ever get. Pay homage to powerful traditions that contribute to your future goals, but show your community a clear path of what "better" looks like to you.

So what does a good North Star look like? Here are some general guidelines:

- Given this document, a new teacher will be able to align his or her daily practice in ways that strengthen the all-school value proposition.

- It is specific enough to guide the development of curriculum and pedagogy without being so proscriptive that it limits the freedom and creativity of individual teachers and administrators to put their personal colors into their practice.

- It explains what is most important to the school community through a relatively few core, value-differentiating themes, rather than trying to include everything that is meaningful to everyone in the community.

- It is long enough to provide clarity without using strings of single-word adjectives whose meaning can be ambiguous.

There are good North Stars that are a few sentences and great North Stars that are a few pages. In contrast to a vision statement, it is not only OK but *preferable* to let your North Star be a bit longer if that is what is needed for clarity. I include a list of example schools, most of which did not start out with the North Star metaphor nor is it referred to as such in their respective schools. Nonetheless, they provide the same guiding point value for the learning practice at their schools (simple searches should take you to the relevant schools and pages, with the caveat that these statements may not live on the respective websites forever!):

- High Tech High Design Principles
- Design 39 Campus Guiding Principles
- IowaBIG Core Design Principles
- Miami Valley School Vision
- Green Vale School Principles of Learning

Once formally adopted, the North Star is a simple, effective, and powerful tool by which your organization can both make and measure change. It gives a guide to where you should look for innovation. It gives you a rubric by which to assess new ideas as possible sources of future value. And it provides at least a first-order frame in which to ask and answer this critical question: *Are we getting closer to our North Star than we were before?*

BIG QUESTIONS FOR YOUR COMMUNITY

1. Does your school have a North Star toward which all members of your team align their practice and professional growth? Is the language of the North Star unambiguous or open to interpretation by each member of the community? How do you know?

2. How might your school start to gather data that can be distilled into a good North Star statement?

3. How does your North Star make your school stand out from other schools?

4. When you have a North Star, how will it be most useful to your school community?

Once your team has created a strong North Star, you have a self-generated tool of shared interest and accountability. Now you can spread the nutrients that will allow the team to thrive in that ecosystem of shared interest. A culture that values innovation will thrive in the wellspring of those nutrients.

CHAPTER 15

Building Cultures of Innovation in Schools

In Chapter 1, we adopted a simple definition of innovation for schools: *Innovation is about creating, finding, and implementing new ideas that add value to the organization in the long term.* For at least the last four decades, the business world has found that innovation is a powerful engine of success. As new technologies in transportation, purchasing, communication, knowledge-sharing, travel, and global economics have lowered the barriers to competition, the world has become "flatter." Organizations are less able to sustain value by merely increasing efficiency at the margin. Value generation increasingly lies in doing something different enough to set your organization apart from your competitors in the minds of the consumer.

For much of those four decades, indeed for most of the last 150 years, schools did not have to deal with the realities of a competitive market. Now we do. So let's dig deeper into the nature of innovation and how to both jump-start and sustain a stable foundation for innovative practices at your school.

First, let's not reinvent the wheel. *The Innovator's DNA* (2011) by Dyer, Gregersen, and Christensen is probably the best and simplest overview of innovation—and one that should be mandatory reading for school leaders. Schools are people-driven organizations, and the authors identify five skills that make innovators different from other people (as shown in Figure 15.1).

Figure 15.1 Innovator Skills

1. **Associating**: The ability to successfully connect seemingly unrelated questions, problems, or ideas from different fields

2. **Questioning**: Finding the right questions to ask, including *why, why not,* and *what if*

3. **Observing**: Scrutinizing common phenomena, particularly the behavior of potential customers. In observing others, they act like anthropologists and social scientists.

4. **Experimenting**: The love of trying and doing, often in the face of repeated "failure"

5. **Networking**: Finding and testing ideas through a network of diverse individuals

Source: Dyer, J., Gregersen, H., and Christiansen, C. (2011). *The innovator's DNA.* Boston, MA: Harvard Business School.

The goal (simple to state; less simple to achieve) then for many schools is *to enhance their overall "innovation DNA."* This chapter is about how to do that with the least amount of traumatic personnel turnover.

Finding and Hiring

There is no easier, better, or less painful way to build innovation capacity in a school than by hiring people who are naturally innovative. This does *not* mean that some people got all of the innovation genes at birth and others will never be good innovators; that is absolutely *not* true. But it *does* mean that innovation is something that comes more naturally to some people than to others or that some people have been able to develop those skills of innovation more deeply than others. By simply hiring educators who are effective innovators, who are interested in trying new things, and who are more comfortable in working with other innovators, school organizations can dramatically enhance their ability to change.

Educators are becoming an increasingly rare species. In many states and regions, the projected deficits for qualified teachers in the next 20 years are frightening. Hiring good teachers is a competition that will only become stiffer in the future. Faced with this, how might your school identify, attract, hire, and retain adults who will strengthen your overall innovation DNA?

One way is to *hire differently* from other schools. The traditional metric (somewhat oversimplified) for hiring a new teacher looks something like this:

- Where did the candidates teach/work before, or if they are new, where did they go to school and get their credential?

- Were they effective in the classroom or the office in their last job?

- Do they know and can they deliver their content and manage their students/employees?

In other words, we have traditionally hired educators based on two factors: pedigree and past success at working within the traditional system. Schools that want to enhance their innovation DNA need to start by adopting a different hiring rubric.

Several years ago, Sammie Cervantez, then-principal of Shell Beach Elementary School on the central California coast, described to me how they hired teachers the previous year. They gathered all of their job applicants in a gymnasium in which they had set up a series of "stations." One station involved a group-design challenge; one required applicants to develop a block of curriculum together; another challenged the team to solve a discipline problem; a fourth was a traditional "group-build" challenge like the well-known marshmallow and pasta problem. A half-dozen principals stood around the edges of the gym and just watched and made notes for a couple of hours. At the end, the applicants were dismissed, and the principals held a "draft." About 80 percent of the top 10 applicants were the same on all of the principals' ranked lists. Without reviewing folders, setting up individual interviews, or scheduling mock teaching time, the principals had all answered the most important hiring questions: *Who do I want to work with, and who will work well with my team?*

"If I have a teacher who is struggling to deliver a bit of curriculum," Sammie said, "or who needs brushing up on her subject, I have all kinds of resources to support her. That problem I can solve. But if I hire people who don't work well together in teams or who are not creative thinkers or who are not comfortable with finding quirky solutions, we are never going to be good at changing how we 'do' school."

Many schools turn over between 5 percent and 10 percent (or more) of their teachers each year due to retirement, natural movement within the district, or moving out of the area. These schools have the opportunity to turn over half of their staff within a five-year window *without having to fire/counsel out anyone.* Since most organizations naturally have 10 percent to 15 percent of "hard chargers" or "natural change agents," this means that in any five-year period, by just changing how and who you hire, you can build a "high innovation DNA" team, filled with growth-mindset teachers and administrators.

Garth Nichols, an educator and thought leader in Toronto, as well as one of my closest partners in accelerating strategic change in schools, suggests some very clear "new rubrics" for hiring in Figure 15.2.

There is, of course, one very big catch: Do these teachers actually exist? The answer to that is "yes, but . . . ." In my last book, *Moving the Rock* (Lichtman, 2017), one of the seven levers for true educational transformation that I identified was the desperate need for our credentialing colleges and universities to ramp up training teachers how to be comfortable with innovation. Schools of education are pathetically slow at making this change, but it is and will happen as more schools and districts demand these skills.

For now, it is a competitive race to find teachers who want to help lead change. Make your school highly visible and attractive to the innovators in the applicant pool. The rising generation of millennials are eager to work with teams who share your values. Innovative educators love working in innovative environments, so the more a school or district is known as a beacon of innovation, the more they will attract "innovation DNA-rich"

Figure 15.2 Interview Questions for the New Hiring Standards

The Old Way	Some New Hiring Standards
Where did the candidates teach/work before, or if they are new, where did they go to school and get their credential?	Can they identify opportunities and challenges for innovation in their past? What challenges and opportunities do they see for your school for innovation?
Were they effective in the classroom or the office in their last job?	In what ways did they measure their effectiveness in the classroom? In what ways did they add value in new ways through their role?
Do they know and can they deliver their content and manage their students/employees?	In what ways are they exploring new pedagogies and technologies to enhance student learning?

applicants. Forming a relationship with local teacher colleges and inserting student teachers into classrooms with known change agents is a great way to identify young starting teachers who will elevate the innovation DNA of your school when hired for a permanent position.

Creating Cultures of Learning

I don't believe in reinventing the wheel, so where strategies have already been effectively translated into "school speak," I am not going to recreate that good work. But this book would not be complete if I ignored a key element of innovative change, which is that *schools are places of human interactions.* Humans lie at the center of learning, and humans are the key to changing them when change is needed.

As I work with schools, I see a common theme repeated: If we fail to support innovation at a very human level, all the rest of the work we did in getting the school on track can disappear almost overnight. Some people, books, and resources that you should access are as follows:

- Julie Wilson has two decades of experience working in corporate entities, higher education, and K–12 organizations. Her book *The Human Side of Changing Education* (2018) outlines effective human-centric tools that educators can use to help themselves and their teams cross bridges of change.

- Ron Ritchardt has been a leader of Harvard's Project Zero, a primary mover of how to convert schools from the outdated Industrial Age model to a place of deeper learning. Ron's book *Creating Cultures of Thinking* (2015) is a primer on how schools are making the shift from organizations that define themselves based on teaching to organizations that are focused on learning.

- *Building Schools 2.0* (2015) by Science Leadership Academy founding principal Chris Lehmann and former SLA teacher Zac Chase provides step-by-step, hallway-by-hallway, and day-to-day vignettes on how a growing, dynamic, co-learning group of educators consistently delivers on a wildly successful, differentiated, schoolwide value proposition.

- *Timeless Learning* (2018) by Ira Socol, Pam Moran, and Chad Ratliff is a book in which all reform-minded educators can find themselves. The authors have decades of experience in diverse public schools, and they add real-life color with stories and voice that come from that rich experience. A reader takes away from this book, "If they can do it, so can I," a personally empowering shift for any prospective education change agent.

To these marvelous resources, and more that I could add and that will be written by the time you are reading this, let me add three suggestions that can help build that foundation of a schoolwide culture of learning (see Figure 15.3).

Figure 15.3 Suggestions for Creating a Culture of Learning

1. **School communities are highly congenial but not collegial enough.** We are afraid of hurting feelings or appearing to have a strong opinion to the point that we fail to support each other as well as we might. To be collegial means to be supportive of your colleagues, which includes being attentive, interested in their work and ideas, and above all, honest. It means asking for and receiving feedback. Schools that struggle with change are those where we find low levels of trust, even among colleagues who have worked together for years or decades. Schools that are able to imagine and act on innovative changes are those where adults share their own growth and learning goals, ask for classroom visits and 360-degree feedback, provide honest feedback to others, and then act upon it with the relish and enthusiasm in which it is provided. There are numerous resources and ideas from practicing educators on how to develop these growth-supporting nutrients on sites like Edutopia and Next Gen Learning.

2. **Innovation rarely happens through traditional top-down hierarchies of decision making.** The world changes too quickly, and the tenure of most school leaders is just too short. Most importantly, systems change when people change, and people change when they have a stake in the change, which happens more when "we" design and deliver something in which "we" find value than when change is mandated from above. Titular school leaders must study and implement ways to *distribute leadership* authority "downward" and across the school. All educators are potential leaders, and when they both know and feel that to be true, value-rich innovation can take off like wildfire.

3. **Many adults in schools, and teachers in particular, fear that once something is *discussed* it is, in fact, *decided*.** As we ask people to become more invested in more strategic ways, to take ownership in delivering on our shared value proposition, we need to be clear about at least three levels of collaborative work: discussion, design, and decision. *Discussions* are just a kickoff point, a chance for diverse groups to share ideas, *some* of which *may* end up leading to a change in the school. *Designing* is about taking that diverse input and creating a first or second prototype and presenting it to others for honest feedback. *Decisions* are taken at appropriate levels, depending on the magnitude of the change. Teams should be very clear when they gather about the purpose of their work: Are we here to discuss, design, or decide?

Jump-Starting Innovation in Schools

Value-rich innovation does not just happen, and it does not always thrive, even in organizations with innovation-rich DNA. And most schools don't have a Silicon Valley–like innovation hyperdrive. Within the context of how schools function in the *real* world, what can you do in order to seed and nurture innovation that may grow to become a systemwide norm?

There are entire libraries devoted to this topic, but I will settle on four simple tactics (see Figure 15.4)

Shout loudly about attempts, successes, and failures. Invite scrutiny, discussion, debate, and feedback. Celebrate and reward those who lead when leading is not necessarily part of their job description.

Figure 15.4 Four Tactics for Jump-Starting Innovation in Schools

1. **Inspire stretch results.** We ask our students to stretch their own work; there was a time (long gone, it seems) when the grade *A* was only given for work that reflected a stretch by the student. The kinds of innovations worth a traditional *A* grade are *almost never* found when we stay within a comfort zone. Dworkin and Spiegel (2016) suggest that we "play under the lights," that we make innovation and appropriate risk-taking a very public focus of the organization. Shout loudly about attempts, successes, and failures. Invite scrutiny, discussion, debate, and feedback. Celebrate and reward those who lead when leading is not necessarily part of their job description. When your educator team knows that strategic design and innovative contributions are rewarded, they are much more likely to stretch for both tangible and intangible brass rings.

2. **Build rich interactions.** As General McChrystal (2015) did with his teams in Iraq, create *many opportunities* for adults to get outside of their own silos and then *give weight* to the work they do. Most educators believe that empathy is a critical skill to teach our students; we can model and practice empathy much better when we spend more time working with, observing, and learning alongside "the other." A legendary high school English teacher once told me that the best day of professional development he ever spent was observing a second-grade classroom, thinking about the pedagogy of effective learning with 7-year-olds, and how those same techniques could be applied to ramp up relevancy and engagement with his high school juniors and seniors. Rich, frequent interactions create the conditions around which naturally innovative people are more likely to spark ideas off one another and that help cautious people value the *opportunities* of change more than the fear it brings.

3. **Dump rigidity.** Our traditional schools have a terrible linearity at the core of the operating system. It tells us that there is *one best way* to do things and that deviating from that path is wrong or even forbidden. We often make the military and business worlds seem chaotically flexible in comparison! Yet we *know* that this is not the way successful people and organizations work, nor is it the way that all students learn best. Increasingly, your customers/families know this as well. Yes, there are some rigid boundary conditions to what we must do in school that are beyond our control. But site-level leaders and even classroom teachers have tremendous autonomy to work within those boundaries. Some schools take the view, for example, that Common Core standards limit their ability to try creative learning practices, while other schools see the standards as highly liberating. One group accepts the past as the boundaries of the future, while the other is eager to press the limits of their autonomy.

4. **Experiment.** Every innovation model ends with "ship it"—produce, try, iterate, and try again. Schools have traditionally been risk averse; the default has been "If we aren't sure, we will wait." We have to shift to "When in doubt, try it out," with the caveat, of course, that safety is always the top priority. When we try new ideas, there is always a point where we have to either continue on the traditional (usually easier) path or pivot to something new and less tested. *Innovative organizations embrace the pivot.* Leaders visibly publicize how they are willing to try new things (and not just with technology). Leaders don't fall in love with their own first solutions but want others to try solve problems from a range of different perspectives before leaping in and deciding that "this is where we will go."

that seem to work well for jump-starting innovation in schools that are based on a framework by Dworkin and Spiegel (2016).

If you are reading this and say to yourself, "But I don't know what that looks like; give me some examples," take heart (and look to the resources in Appendix II). A decade ago, there were a handful of schools that we could point to as exemplars of great innovation. Today, there are hundreds and so many more each year that any particular citation would be out of date before I write it. The exemplars of this kind of innovation-rich fertilization are cropping up everywhere, probably near you.

Tactic #4: When in doubt, try it out.

BIG QUESTIONS FOR YOUR COMMUNITY

1. How might you shift your hiring practices to identify, hire, and retain people who are eager to embrace innovation?

2. How is growth mindset and the development of a learning culture directly tied to your employee evaluation system?

3. What steps can you take as a school to inspire people to make "stretches" and to foster rich interactions and experimentation?

Strong ecosystems are diverse ecosystems.
School cultures that are sustainably innovative
and growth oriented need cross-pollination
with the outside world. This does not mean
that schools should look like businesses! It
means that we know and value learning—and
that means learning from the best, wherever
we find it.

At a time when we are all trying to predict an uncertain future, we can learn a great deal about how effective organizations work with a look backward. Frederic Laloux (*Reinventing Organizations*, 2016) researched the evolution of a wide range of organizations over 100,000 years of human history and where they are headed today. He describes a surprisingly simple scaffold of organizational evolution, playfully identified with colors:

- **Infrared** organizations: They are small bands of people with limited development of the individual ego.

- **Magenta** organizations: They are tribes of a few hundred people held together by daily needs and a magical/mythical understanding of the world around them.

- **Red** organizations: They feel the constant exercise of power by the chief to keep troops in line; fear is the glue of the organization. They are highly reactive, with short-term focus. They are typified by gangs, Mafias, and tribal militias.

- **Amber** organizations: These have highly formal roles within a hierarchical pyramid with top-down command. Stability is valued above all. The future is seen as repetition of the past. They are typified by the Catholic church, military, most government agencies, and traditional public school systems.

- **Orange** organizations: They are modern, and their goal is to beat the competition and achieve profit or growth. Innovation is the key to staying ahead. They are typified by multinational companies, social impact nonprofits, and charter schools.

- **Green** organizations: They are postmodern and focus on culture and empowerment to achieve extraordinary employee performance. They are typified by culture-driven organizations (frequently cited examples are Southwest Airlines and Ben and Jerry's).

Laloux identifies one more category, **Teal**, that is starting to evolve today. Like many school communities, Teal organizations, view themselves as places of deep introspection, sharing, consensus and approval, collegiality, trust, passionate commitment to the development of character and wisdom, and the strength of personal connections more than a fountain of dogma. A relatively small number of for-profit companies can be classified as Teal, but many school communities see themselves as naturally Teal-like in many ways.

Traditional schools are still stuck in Amber. More innovative challengers that have evolved over the last few decades, such as charter schools, stepped up to Orange in order to carve out a piece of the marketplace. Innovative schools today almost all exhibit strong Green tendencies. The fact that you are reading this book and that you want to move your school or district to maintain powerful relevancy for your community suggests that you see the value of Green or Teal organizations in today's education system.

Lessons From Silicon Valley

While we are in a new, competitive market for students, schools are decidedly *unlike* most businesses in many ways. Most schools, thankfully, are not formed in order to make a profit for shareholders. We serve children for whom we feel a powerful responsibility, not for *our* benefit, but to help *them* find future success and happiness. Schools are a core part of the social fabric *in which we participate*, more like churches, voting, arts, and sports than like the businesses that sell *to* us.

Yet in an increasingly competitive environment, there are powerful lessons we can learn from for-profit companies that succeed in times of evolving markets and changing consumer needs. Since the 1970s, there has been no more powerful center of innovation gravity on the planet than Silicon Valley, a place, ethos, and culture that has impacted the lives of virtually every human in profound ways. Why is Silicon Valley the Magic Kingdom of innovation, and what lessons can K–12 schools learn about how innovation succeeds in times of rapid change? Here are three indicators: *density, fluidity*, and *strategic focus*.

Effective Density

Silicon Valley has developed a remarkable *density* of talent during the technology revolution. It started at Stanford University and quickly spread through garages and offices between San Francisco and San Jose and then across the Bay to the University of California at Berkeley. That density allowed many of the characteristics of the Valley model to evolve: *frequent formal and informal connections, mobility of workers* from company to company, and an *openness and sharing of ideas* between people who might fiercely compete in the workplace and also be close friends after hours. The stories of technology pioneers like Apple cofounder Steve Wozniak sharing his first designs for a primitive homemade computer motherboard with a bunch of budding computer nerds at informal meet-ups are legend. Passionate innovators feed off each other, and they need to connect frequently in order to share their passions.

> Passionate innovators feed off each other, and they need to connect frequently in order to share their passions.

Individuals in schools, our potential innovators, have traditionally lacked access to this density of connections. We are open and sharing with our ideas . . . when we happen to interact. We work closely by each other, but few of us connect frequently beyond the silos where we are stuck most of the day: our classroom, office, department, grade level, or campus. There are many, many educators and schools, but we lack *effective density* in terms of the critical connections that lead to real innovation.

Schools that innovate effectively proactively increase effective density. You and your colleagues have many connection pathways available to you: increased classroom visits, instructional rounds, social media, EdCamps, local and regional miniconferences, education Twitter chats, and critical friend networks to name some. Take 10 minutes in your next faculty meeting to map individual and collective professional connections. Then, brainstorm cheap, frequent, fast ways to increase density of those connections both internally within the school and externally to the greater world of education and beyond. You will find a world of opportunities to build the density of connections—to expand the learning networks of your team—in ways that do not add dramatically to their workload. Learn from your students; they are vastly more networked in their lives than you are in yours! You will find that many educators *want* to be more connected to colleagues who are trying new and better ways to engage their students; they just don't know how to make those connections.

Fluidity

Another key characteristic of Silicon Valley innovation is the remarkably *fluid movement of both people and ideas*. People move from one company to another, taking and sharing ideas, progress, success, and failure as they go. These movements create an ever-roiling stew of creative innovation as groups find new ways to merge ideas at the margins of their respective experiences. One of the most powerful catalysts to this movement of people and their ideas is the *tolerance for failure*. Not only is failure in the last job accepted in the Valley, but it is often a prerequisite of future employment. Companies recognize that a person who has tried and failed, often multiple times, has a far more valuable mindset and field of understanding than one who has played it safe or colored within all of the lines.

Successfully innovating schools empower fluidity of movement. Traditional schools are static organizations with many teachers who have taught in the same room, grade level, department, division, school, or district for their entire careers. For much of this time, they have not been empowered or expected to take a risk. They teach the same syllabus year after year, in spite of changes in the world—dramatic changes in the way students learn today relative to even a decade ago and revolutionary understandings of how the brain actually works. Risk is anathema to these teachers for good reason: If they have failed or performed poorly according to rigid organizational practices, there is a lot of downside and little upside to taking a risk.

Increasing fluidity does not require that teachers constantly leave their schools and move to another. *Movement of mind and practice can take place within a single school*. At one school I visited, I was told that teachers *almost never* meet with colleagues outside of their department or curriculum development team. This is an absurd reality in many schools, but it is easy to change. Schools can easily and quickly adopt a new set of practices that will draw them closer to the proven best practices of creative innovation (see Figure 16.1).

Figure 16.1   Practices That Will Draw You Closer to Creative Innovation

- Limit the number of years a teacher stays in one course or grade level. Reward those who move more frequently; they are demonstrating a valuable growth mindset.
- Empower, promote, require, and celebrate risk-taking in the creation of new programs, use of pedagogy, and curriculum.
- Require, celebrate, and reward teachers who join and lead in professional networks on social media with colleagues from beyond the school or district.
- Create annual or semiannual "Teachers Teach Teachers" events on professional development days. Redirect the money you pay to consultants on these days to reward teachers who prepare and deliver active-learning workshops for their peers.
- Research the growing number of inexpensive or free practitioner-led conferences and gatherings, and motivate teacher teams to attend one near you.
- Hire new teachers who have a proven track record of trying something new.

It is easy to help teachers and administrators move outside their comfort zones. It may be uncomfortable, but it's not hard. And isn't this what we want our students to do? How can we expect them to push into discomfort, to take an intellectual risk, if we don't show them how?

Strategic Focus

Silicon Valley is a hive of rapid product development. Companies compete to imagine, design, test, modify, and then reject or double down on what consumers want and need. There are three basic types of companies in this highly competitive high technology market (Jaruzelski & Dehoff, 2010):

- There are the **"tech drivers,"** companies that seek to invent a new technology or tweak an existing technology in ways that will drive new interest and sales. Schools and educators that fall into this group are constantly on the lookout for a new technology, course offering, or teaching methodology that will improve student performance, which attracts more families to choose them.

- There are **"market readers,"** companies that use data and closely watch competitors to divine the direction of market interest and get there in advance of the competition with a new product or service. Schools that fall into this category seek a competitive advantage relative to local alternatives, regardless of what is happening in a broader geographic or educational context. They may even be willing to sacrifice long-term learning outcomes in order to meet short-term market demand.

- And there are the **"need seekers,"** companies that try to understand what consumers really want today and in the future and to create products and services that meet those needs and desires.

The 2010 study by Booz and Company (Jaruzelski & Dehoff, 2010) found that those companies that define their strategy as "need seekers" *consistently outperformed the others* and were much more effective at both the ideation and conversion stages of innovation. These companies *directly engage their customers* to find out what they really want and how best to provide it, regardless of legacy assumptions about what the market of products and services might look like. They engage in truly expansive thinking and are willing to test ideas that just flat out scare others.

> Companies that define their strategy as "need seekers" *consistently outperformed the others* and were much more effective at both the ideation and conversion stages of innovation.

Schools in the past have not been "need seekers." For the most part, we have assumed that what has worked well for our customers in the past will work pretty well in the future ("That's how I learned, and I turned out OK!"). Most educators rarely engage in deep conversation with their customers about their needs and desires for education. In fact, we rarely engage in deep conversation with our *own educators* about what great education really looks like!

Figure 16.2 Finding the Sweet Spot

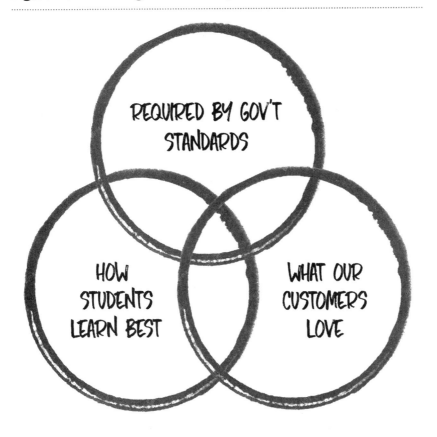

REQUIRED BY GOV'T STANDARDS

HOW STUDENTS LEARN BEST

WHAT OUR CUSTOMERS LOVE

Schools that understand "need seeking" also frequently, passionately, and authentically engage with their community of stakeholders to find the Venn overlap seen in Figure 16.2 of what is required by government standards, what we as educators know leads to good learning, and what our customers want and need. "Need seeking" does not mean you follow the latest trends just to be seen as cutting edge. The sweet spot of this Venn diagram is just that: a place where *all three* of these driving forces overlap.

BIG QUESTIONS FOR YOUR COMMUNITY

1. What "color" is your organization, and what can you do to elevate from that color toward Orange, Green, or Teal?

2. How does the "color" of your school align with the "innovation DNA" of your school?

3. How might you increase the effective density of creative interactions for your people, both inside and outside of school?

4. How might you foster and reward fluidity of movement across traditional school boundaries and silos?

You are building a value-oriented team and
culture at your school. Do you just wing it
when you are building a house? When you are
cooking dinner? When you are teaching? No!
The tools we have discussed so far are only
valuable if they produce the results you need
for your school to thrive over time. And for
that, we need to measure in ways that we have
not done in the past.

CHAPTER 17

Measuring Innovation

District and site leaders need tools to measure how well their teams are doing. Every school governing board wants to know how to measure innovation. How do we know that the time, energy, money, and skill-building involved in this cultural shift are *working*? These are important and legitimate questions. The last thing schools need is another vague initiative that might or might not be working.

I want to be crystal clear here: There is no innate guarantee that "innovation" leads to better student test scores. (Some innovative schools have seen increases in test scores; others have not.) If you measure school success largely or wholly by student test scores, then you should spend a lot of time preparing students for tests. If you are going to measure school success by how well you excite and engage your users with the strength of your value proposition, then you need to measure the actual *process of innovation* itself. You have plenty of other rubrics from which to choose when it comes to measuring student performance.

While the rubrics are evolving all the time, there are some places that school leaders can start today. Langdon Morris, in his book *The Innovation Master Plan* (2011), cites a dozen measures that companies can use to determine the extent to which they are *actually* innovative. Many of these measurements sound "corporate" to those in education nonprofits, but the roots of success are both applicable and achievable in schools, and all of them can be measured. (In Figure 17.1, the headings of each are from Morris; the descriptions are mine.)

Figure 17.1 Assessing Innovation

- **Outputs of innovation significantly enhance the brand.** *Innovation*, by definition, is the implementation of new ideas that build organizational value as measured through the viewpoint of our customers. Ask *How do our innovative pilots directly align with a strong and differentiated value proposition?* Positive results of innovation include when students, teachers, and parents increasingly can articulate the relationship between new programs and practices and your North Star, as well as an increase in your school's Net Promoter Score.

- **Customer opinions improve steadily and significantly.** Sustainable value is not based on anecdotes about a few top students or a handful of exceptional teachers. Innovative schools broadly and frequently sample their customers

(Continued)

Figure 17.1 (Continued)

about how well students are engaged with their learning. Ask your stakeholders *What does great learning look like to you?* or *Tell us about at time when our school failed to meet your needs.* Positive results include when parents and students draw clear lines in their stories between the school's North Star and their own daily experience. Conversations in the parking lot of your school are the conversations you want parents to have: positive and generative.

- **The innovation system engages a large and growing ecosystem of external partners.** Remember that the two big drivers of creativity are risk-taking and connectivity. Schools have been remarkably isolated from the world around them. Creating frequent and numerous opportunities to interact with external partners both inside and outside of education is hugely fertile ground for school innovation. Ask *How might we become deeply engaged or embedded with community resources that will amplify our vision . . . maybe right here on campus?* A positive result of this interaction is increasing numbers of formal and informal partnerships with people and organizations beyond the school that contribute to desired learning outcomes.

- **A significant increase in the number of attractive, new internally sourced opportunities.** Innovative organizations build and maintain a diversified portfolio of new ideas that *may* grow into value-generating learning experiences. Schools that support one or two isolated brushfires of creative innovation may feel good that they are incubating change, but odds are they don't have enough creative ideas in the pipeline. Ask a diverse group of stakeholders *How are we pushing ourselves beyond our comfort zone in ways that are directly tied to learning?* A positive result is that the range and number of pilot projects aligned to the North Star is rising over time.

- **Speed of innovation project completion increases year after year.** Schools are notorious for taking a long time to move from idea to practice. This flies straight in the face of what we know about the relationships of fast ideation, iteration, and successful innovation. School leaders must become more comfortable with trying something with no guarantee of success and then iterating or moving on to other ideas on a much more frequent cycle. Ask *If the change we seek is important, can we accelerate the timeline of trial, iteration, and implementation?* A positive result is when the school demonstrates that the time to go from idea to implementation is decreasing relative to even a few years ago.

- **Number of people participating in innovation projects increases year after year.** Like frequency, *density* of innovation is an indicator of success. If one person or a few small groups are seen as "the innovative types" or that it is "their" job, the school is not building a sustainable capacity to innovate. Ask *Is growth-minded innovation a hope or an expectation at our school?* A positive result is that an increasing number of people are creating or participating in pilot projects—not because they are told to, but because they want to.

Figure 17.1 is just a starter list; there are many other suggested ways to measure innovation, and more will have been created by the time you read this.

The Innovation Portfolio

Ultimately, you have to ask *How do we know that what we are doing is succeeding?* If we accept the validity of the strategy–value–innovation equation, then innovation becomes a process that we need to measure in at least two important ways:

- **First**, do the innovations we adopt lead to a more sustainable school that is fulfilling its mission?

- **Second**, regardless of the success of any one innovative change in our school, is our *process of innovation* gaining in health? Are we building *capacity* for sustained innovation?

Innovation is like any other investment in our future (see Figure 17.2). Anyone with a retirement account (hopefully) understands that neither placing all of your money under a mattress or betting it all on the ponies at the racetrack is a great idea. The best long-term investments, like your 401(k), contain a distribution of low-risk/lower reward and higher-risk/higher-potential reward opportunities. So one simple way to look at the health of innovation in your department, school, or district is to simply place various pilot projects or ideas on a risk-versus-reward plot. Those that land in the lower-left quadrant are "low-hanging fruit." They won't lead to immediate major changes, but they don't really require much effort or risk. We can think of these innovations in terms of "If we could just wake up tomorrow

Figure 17.2 Risk/Return Trade-Off

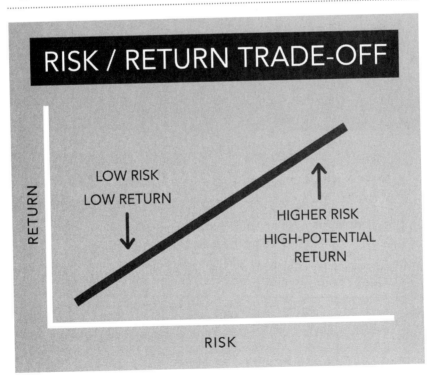

and make these changes, which we want and think are great, we would," then just do it.

Items that land increasingly toward the upper-right corner of the graph take more resources, planning, buy-in, and, usually, time to implement. These generally include major revisions to the primary elements of the school operating system: how we use time and physical space, shifting from single-subject to interdisciplinary learning, how we group students, and so on.

Like your 401(k) accounts, you want a balance in your school's "innovation portfolio." If your plot is void in the upper-right quadrant, it means that you have not pushed your thinking beyond a relatively safe comfort zone, and the likelihood of making a significant change in the school is small.

If your program or school is losing students or if you think that the future might change in unpredictable ways—and even if your school is doing well now—you can't afford to place all of your eggs in the safe, lower-left quadrant on this graph. Schools and districts with the best chance of long-term success are those that continue to generate innovative pilots, some of which will succeed and others of which will fail, across this risk–reward spectrum.

The Innovation Tracker

The Morris measurements of innovation I outlined in Figure 17.1 are largely *qualitative* measures, which are every bit as valid as *quantitative* measures. But we also can measure the progress of a school as an innovative organization using *objective* data tracked *over time*. This framework, first published as the Innovation Benchmarking Report in 2015, creates a simple table to measure the progress of specific ideas and pilots over time, as well as to use objective criteria to measure that progress (see Figure 17.3).

Figure 17.3 Rubric for Progress of Innovations Over Time

	Ideation Stage	Research Stage	Prototype Stage	Pilot Stage	Scaling/ Implementation Stage
How much are we investing?					
How many ongoing projects are at this stage?					
How long has the project been at this stage?					
How many projects have advanced?					
Which group or individual generated each idea?					

By updating this simple tracker once a year, your school can map progress using objective data. A Silicon Valley start-up would have a very different set of tracker data than an established, successful school, and a school or district struggling to attract or retain students will have very different tracker data than a school that is not facing as many of these challenges today. As an industry, we don't have enough data points on this kind of measurement tool to be able to call out "best practices," but those will grow over time, so why not start measuring now?

Where Should *Your* School Focus for Effective Innovation?

Educators are used to focusing on *learning outcomes*, not the process of organizational innovation. When we start a conversation about innovation, many of us feel that we are walking into a swamp without a compass. How do we start and stay on a path of change that has the best chance of leading to long-term sustainability? We can't be engaged in high-level strategic evaluations all the time! What *daily practices* can we encourage and engage in at our school that will most likely nurture a culture of value-rich innovation?

In competitive markets, there are no guarantees, but we can learn from other successful organizations, even if they are not involved in education. They have been down these paths many times, and we need to learn their lessons. The Business Performance Innovation Network (2015) published data from a survey of 200 CEOs about what drives innovation in their organizations. Some of the highlights align very closely to what I think we are seeing in effectively innovating schools (see Figure 17.4).

Figure 17.4 Drivers of Effective Innovation Across Many Organizations

- **The three most important drivers of innovation are**
  - CEO-driven cultural commitment
  - Reduction of silos and obstacles to new thinking
  - Better customer feedback
- **Innovation is needed most in the areas of**
  - Engaging and sustaining customers
  - Building culture and mindsets that support a willingness to embrace change

(Continued)

Figure 17.4 (Continued)

- **Innovation resources are best spent on**
  - Defining innovation-based strategies and *specific* projects
  - Shifting organizational DNA in the direction of innovation
  - Supporting bottom-up ideation
- **Innovation becomes actionable and accountable by**
  - Making it part of the enterprise strategy
  - Developing innate skills and talents within the current workforce
  - Creating simple measures and metrics of creative innovation
- **The biggest obstacles to innovation are**
  - Self-preservation of roles, interests, and positions
  - Management politics
  - Organizational structures that are resistant to change
- **We can best encourage innovation through**
  - Better evaluation and rewards
  - Fast-tracking "entrepreneurship"
  - Clearly defining innovation goals and policies
- **The most important qualities of change agents who will lead innovation are**
  - Willingness to challenge traditional thinking
  - Ability to marry innovation with strategy
  - Their ability to activate their colleagues

Do not try to incorporate or tackle all of these at once! You will blow a personal head gasket and make everyone around you crazy. Choose a few, and ask members of your leadership team to also choose a few. Make these a centerpiece of your team's annual goal-setting and review process. Collectively, you will be recentering your organizational focal point on practices that actually support innovative thinking and growth.

Strangely Great Innovation Metrics for Schools

In the mid-2000s, I exchanged a few e-mails with Keith Evans, a leader in American independent schools. He sent me five quirky metrics that he had imagined could be used to measure innovation at a school.

Ignited by his utterly outside-the-box thinking, I added four of my own (see Figure 17.5). We tweaked them a bit back and forth, and for the life of me, I don't know which were originally his and which were mine. I am pretty sure that few schools are formally using any of these, but you might want to try and, more importantly, come up with and share some of your own!

Figure 17.5 "Strange" Metrics to Measure Innovation

1. **Organizational Velocity**: A calculation of the average speed at which a worthy new idea travels the path to implementation—a notoriously sluggish pace in most academic environments.

2. **Curiosity Index**: A simple subtraction function that measures whether a student is more curious upon graduation than at enrollment (related to the **Intellectual Curiosity Quotient**, which is a predictor of this Index). It calculates the ratio of time spent by students in class asking questions to the time spent answering questions. Any resulting fraction greater than 1.0 is a mark of an intellectually curious learning environment.

3. **Obsolescence Ratio:** The ratio of legacy practices to new methods employed in the leadership and organization of the school. This metric is sometimes measured by the number of familiar experiences a parent has in navigating the school with two children at least five years apart.

4. **Anti-Tech Innovation Coefficient:** A measure of the number of changes in classroom instruction that do *not* include use of a new technology as a measure of the creative intelligence of a teacher.

5. **Faculty and Staff Performance Discussion Event Horizon:** An easily measurable metric where the only question posed about faculty and staff evaluation is this: "What percentage of our employees is performing at or above the expected standard?" If the answer is 95 percent or greater, everyone moves on to more productive conversation. If the answer is fewer than 95 percent, the performance and quality of the faculty and staff becomes the topic of the first objective in the strategic plan.

6. **Strategy Corruption Quotient:** Assumes an inverse correlation between the size of a strategic plan and the quality of the strategic thinking in it.

7. **Silo Scale:** The ratio of the time and energy spent working alone versus collaborating.

8. **Coordinates of the Intellectual Campus:** Uses GPS to measure the extent to which the physical boundaries of a campus define the boundaries for learning. This metric would also account for new ideas and perspectives brought to the physical campus by outside speakers and visitors as well as the use of technology to reach beyond campus boundaries.

9. **The $F = A$ Paradox:** The measure of that portion of the curriculum where the greatest risks and failures are given the greatest reward. Absent this metric, all that stuff about learning from our mistakes is a lot of hot air and bad transcripts.

BIG QUESTIONS FOR
YOUR COMMUNITY

1. Which measures of innovation might be the most useful for increasing the appetite for innovation within your school community?

2. Which "innovation killers" do you readily recognize at your school? What opportunities are there to overcome these challenges?

3. Where can you increase attention, focus, or resources to most positively impact a culture of innovation at your school?

4. What quirky measures of innovation can you brainstorm to add to the Strangely Great Innovation Metrics?

The work of transforming a school to become irresistible to families in a time of rapid change comes with obstacles. The road is never as smooth as we would like it to be. But the good news is that we know what most of the obstacles are, and we have plenty of evidence that schools with very similar conditions as yours are finding their way over, around, and through many of them.

CHAPTER 18

Inevitable Obstacles

This book has been about solutions, but the road is not without obstacles. Each school, town, and district in America, and indeed around the world, is different. Each has a different mix of people, challenges, and opportunities. There are some obstacles to change that are found at most (if not all) schools. We can either stipulate to these ahead of time and get them into a "parking lot" in our creative strategy, or we can spend precious months or years wringing our hands and arguing the same points. I suggest the former. Raise them up; call them out; recognize that they are problems with which you will have to deal; agree that some of them are just not going to go away and that *your job is to solve the problems you can solve* with effective, creative strategies.

The three most commonly cited obstacles to change in *any* organization are *fear* of the less known, *inertia* (particularly if the organization has been successful in the past), and *aversion to risk*. The PA Consulting Group, in their surveys of business leaders, suggests that more than half of great ideas fail for reasons that could have been avoided. The five most commonly cited *innovation killers* in their surveys are the following (Chandraker, Houmes, Hogg, & Reilly, 2018, pp. 13–14):

- Fear
- Lack of focus on real innovation
- "Engine failure" (the failure of their system to support real innovation)
- Misjudgment about the potential return on investment
- Lack of willingness to invest in something that did not have a proven track record of success

To counter these prevailing obstacles that lie within many or most organizations, Chandraker and colleagues (2018) suggest key strands to the profile of an innovation leader. None of us is going to magically become this person, but from the classroom to the boardroom, there are certain DNA elements that we need to find, hire, retain, and support (see Figure 18.1).

The key to managing these obstacles is to bring them to the surface—to recognize the role they play in the emotions, structures, culture, and processes of the school. Most schools I have visited have never had community-wide conversations about the nature of risk or how to overcome the fear of change or how simple changes to your daily routines can overcome inertia

Figure 18.1 Tips for Being an Innovation Leader

....

Tip #1: Strive to be an innovation leader; don't settle for benchmark "average."
Tip #2: Back a few high-potential, risky ideas.
Tip #3: Learn quickly from mistakes. Put innovation at the heart of your
culture and mission.

Source: Chandraker, A., Houmes, H., Hogg, J., and Reilly, C. (2018). Innovation as unusual. Retrieved from https://www.paconsulting.com/globalassets/downloads/pa-innovation-report -2016.pdf

with relatively little upset to the community. The mere process of *discussing* these obstacles, and rapid design-based ideation about how to get around and through them, is what builds cultural capacity for change.

Then, *hang on* to the discussion about things such as fear and risk aversion. They are not going to go away on their own! Just like going to the weight room for a group of athletes, we have to activate the cultural muscles that defeat these obstacles and free us to collectively perform in ways we have not in the past.

Where We Use Our Resources

The best that I can figure, schools have just five resources: *time, physical space, money, people,* and *knowledge.* Many of those resources are fixed, but some are flexible; many of us can't, for example, build a new building or campus, but we can reconfigure classrooms. Maybe we can't change the start and end of the school day, but we have complete control over how we use the time in between. Maybe we can't hire from outside the district before hiring from within, but we can retool our personnel selection routines. Maybe we can only buy textbooks from an approved list, but we can also create our own learning materials from free, open-educational resources. Maybe we have to meet state standards, but we have a great deal of latitude in the pedagogy and practices we employ in order to meet those standards.

I have asked the following question to tens of thousands of teachers, administrators, and parents: *What is the one thing educators want more of?* I have *never yet* heard a single word other than *time.* No matter what challenges your school organization is facing, it will help accelerate your collective work to throw out a big sign that says something like "Yep; we don't have enough time or money to do what we want, and neither does any other school, so let's park that for now and come back to it when we have decided what it is that we really need and want to do."

The fact is that once schools set their value-rich priorities, they *do* find resources like time. There *are* schools, just like yours, that *have* found ways to give their teachers time to collaborate in teams; time to design learning experiences with their students; time for deeply engaging projects; time for authentic narrative assessments that help students more than letter grades; time to coach small groups of students along personalized learning paths. The schools that have created these opportunities do not have more *total time* than others, and they did not discard core elements of good learning. Their students perform as well or better on standardized tests. They have just decided to break apart and rebuild an operating system that was not meeting their highest aspirations. They choose to use time differently, and so can you.

> Once schools set their value-rich priorities, they *do* find resources like time. Schools just like yours have found time for teachers to collaborate in teams, design learning experiences with students, give authentic narrative assessments, and coach personalized student learning.

What We Can't Control

Every school is bound by some sets of rules over which they have little or no control. These vary by district, state, boards, community standards, and more handbooks than any of us want to know or understand. Many of these rules and standards are in place to protect our students, teachers, and other stakeholders. Some of them are informal traditions that have outlived their original intended purposes and just refuse to die. We want the latter to topple, but some have such deep roots that it seems we just can't weed them out, even when we know they are obstructing good learning practices.

Standardized tests feel like a monster we can't control. Testing is a valuable tool in education; few educators would disagree. Testing that grew over decades through some monstrous irradiation, that absorbs huge amounts of learning time with few improvements in learning outcomes, has limited schools' and individual teachers' abilities to create more engaging classrooms and to *innovate* on behalf of students who need to learn deeply, not in order to take a test. In some states, the rules about testing are so politically hard-wired into the system that the likelihood of changing them, and the effort to do so in any reasonable time frame, seems beyond our capacity at classroom, site, and district levels.

I don't advocate just giving in; the long battles against overtesting have yielded some successes. But you have to prioritize your energies on a risk–reward basis. Figure out what you *really* can't control, and don't overspend time and energy tilting at those windmills. Some of them will topple as they become increasingly irrelevant. In the meantime, gather community support around the things that you *can control* and build momentum by making those changes sooner rather than later. Celebrate your early wins. You will find opportunities to coexist with suboptimal rules in ways that meet faster-evolving customer needs and at the same time build confidence around the fact that *change is possible.*

> Gather community support around the things that you *can control* and build momentum by making those changes sooner rather than later.

Yep, College Admission Is a Real Problem

At nearly every school I have ever visited, deeper learning is showcased, supported, tolerated, promoted, or growing much more in lower grade levels than in high schools, and the reason given is always the same: college admission. There is no doubt whatsoever that traditional metrics for college admission were born from and continue to reflect an industrial measurement of "success." It is darned hard to get school communities to accept or enthusiastically support changes to the K–12 system when there is no guarantee that those changes will be supported in the college admission process.

Despite some very promising efforts like "Turning the Tide" and the Mastery Transcript Consortium (if you don't know those, look them up!), colleges are proving glacially slow in changing their actual admission practices. The reality is that colleges are faced with the same evolutionary pressures that are forcing K–12 to engage in entirely new genres of value proposition, and we don't have a perfect crystal ball of where those pressures will drive college admission practices in the future.

There is every indication that, over time, many—or perhaps most—colleges will admit students based on a different set of standards than they do today. Colleges are faced with financial challenges that will force them to either change their own fundamental operating systems or close the doors. During this period of evolution, there are no perfect answers, other than to continue pushing colleges to practice what they are preaching and to direct your students to apply to colleges that actually value their individual learning accomplishments. Over time, this market pressure will force colleges to change, just as market pressures from parents are driving change for many K–12 schools.

I have found little evidence to support the myth that high schools that change some of their traditional practices that support deeper or more personalized learning and authentic assessments or that deemphasize Advanced Placement courses are hurting their students' college choices. In fact, I hear more stories each year of colleges, particularly the most selective colleges, offering admission to some students precisely *because* they have completed a more unique, student-directed learning pathway during their high school years. If we project these curves out 20 years, it seems a lock that college admission will be less of an obstruction to K–12 innovation than it is today. In the meantime, we deal with VUCA (volatile, uncertain, complex, and ambiguous) world.

Parent Expectations

Parents expect schools to provide everything from a good academic education and college preparation to social services, health care, a place to play, a secure facility for 10 hours a day, and the development of strong character and values. Being the "best" at all of these is impossible for any organization.

I have found two ways that schools can successfully work with, though likely never completely meet, the breadth of parental expectations. The first, as we have discussed, is to create many more opportunities to both listen to what parents say and then gently help them to wrestle with the realities of resource limits. Much of this discussion is within school leaders' control. Garth Nichols encourages us to "create spaces for parents and students to meaningfully engage and provide effective feedback. Schools can host their own 'Parking Lot' discussions and 'Co-Curricular Participation' evenings to solicit feedback. Schools can do more than just ask 'What do you think?'; they have the ability to create laser-focused opportunities to engage their stakeholders."

Not everyone will walk away from these activities satisfied; some people really do expect the impossible. But others begin to better understand both the trade-offs that schools face and also the dissonance that we all feel when the foundations of traditional school are shifting due to forces beyond our control.

Second, remember the most powerful tool you have: You are educators—you know how to create the conditions within which people, including parents, learn well. Your parents are able to learn about the challenges your schools face and the opportunities that arise from those challenges, if you educate them. Use a logic model for what you want your parents to know and feel in several years that is different than it is today, and then, develop a "curriculum" to help them get to those outcomes. The results, as with any good learning, won't happen in one parent meeting or one year. Changing our schools will be an ongoing, sustained process in order to bring together that overlap of what a community needs and what your school can, must, and should provide.

Finding Great Teachers

Periods of evolution are rarely smooth. Needs and resources don't match up nicely. This is the case for schools now. We need teachers who are comfortable with student-centered, deeper-learning pedagogy and curricula, and we need administrators who know how to lead and nurture organization-wide change. Unfortunately, most of our teachers are being trained at colleges and universities that have not transitioned to a new paradigm, and most of our administrators have not taken business school classes in organizational-change leadership.

In *Moving the Rock* (Lichtman, 2017), I devoted two chapters to these problems. It will be years, and probably a decade or more, before our teacher colleges are turning out a steady supply of teachers who are trained to excel in a more dynamic, shifting school setting. Our administrators still don't have access to the kind of business management knowledge that is widely available in the for-profit word. What can teachers and school site and district leaders do in the meantime?

Figure 18.2 speaks to some of the big obstacles with which almost every school has to deal. There are many more; some are common, such as aging facilities, student discipline, and constantly changing technologies. Others are specific to each school, such as the incredible challenges faced by educators serving students living in poverty. None of these are trivial, but it definitely helps if we can surface at least some of the obstacles we face and name them. Then, like the powerful stream of Taoist water that encounters seemingly immovable stones, we creatively, incessantly flow over, around, and under, and erode them over time.

Figure 18.2 Tips for Finding Great Teachers

1. **Look to your current team.** Do you have some members who really want to bust a new move in their practice but maybe have been unwilling to come forward? Which group, if given some highly visible support and encouragement, would be willing to act as that critical nucleus of change? How can your school system add fuel to *their* natural passions? How can *they* become community ambassadors/communicators? How can *they* be positioned to lead others who might be timid or unsure?

2. **Don't wait for others to deliver a new cohort of teachers**, wrapped in a bow, ready to transform the school culture at the start of each new year. The system is way behind in terms of future-leaning educators, so you have to be proactive in finding new members of your team who have the "innovation DNA" we discussed in Chapter 15. In addition to the novel hiring practices we discussed, seek out those graduate schools of education that *are* leading the way in training their teachers to be more flexible and student-focused. Meet with your local teacher colleges and build up internship programs, linking graduate students with your most forward-leaning teachers. Create a pipeline from those colleges that *are* changing their training practices directly to your school or district so you get "pick-of-the-litter" new hires every year.

3. **Make your school highly visible on a national level.** Encourage your leading change agents to blog, tweet, and present at local, regional, state, and national conferences. Host a "Teachers Teach Teachers" day at your school and invite regional teachers to attend. Connect with organizations like Edutopia that have a broad and deep footprint and who are looking for exemplars to share. Let the world know that your school or district is leading in some very tangible way and that you want to find and support like-minded, change-oriented educators who want to disrupt the status quo. It is remarkable how quickly word gets out via the social media pathways today. You will find that innovative educators will start seeking your school or district out because they want to be on a future winning team.

BIG QUESTIONS FOR YOUR COMMUNITY

1. What are some obstacles to change that have frustrated you over the past few years? How might your team begin to overcome them in ways that help you get closer to your North Star?

2. What are you passionate about changing at your school that the community team can actually control . . . even if perhaps they have not felt in total control of that in the past?

3. How might you use your knowledge and skills as a team of educators to help other members of the broader community understand and support your core North Star goals, even if those are nontraditional?

4. What times for engagement—for teachers and students and parents—can be repurposed or tweaked to help you get closer to your North Star?

I'm not sure who first proffered this advice, but it's good: There is a reason that race-car drivers, hurtling around a track at 200 miles per hour, focus on the middle-top section of their windshield, not on the bottom third. The faster you travel, the less valuable it is to look at the ground immediately in front of you and the more important it is to focus farther ahead.

CHAPTER

19

Pushing Our Horizons

When I left my house in the early fall of 2012, I had an energy-efficient Prius, a full tank of gas, GPS on my phone, some spare clothes, a few golf clubs, permission from my wife, and an approximate schedule of schools around the country to visit over the next three months. As far as I could tell, no one had ever visited more than 60 schools in 90 days and reported on what those communities thought about the future of education, the obstacles they were facing, and the solutions that might be percolating in their classrooms, offices, and boardrooms.

Flash forward seven years, and the level of connectivity among K–12 change leaders has literally exploded. Ted Dintersmith (2018) has reported on transforming schools in all 50 states. A half dozen other leading educators I met during that trip in 2012 have published their own books, sharing key strategies of how schools and districts can change everything from the use of time and physical classroom space to leadership practices, human team development, and community demand for relevant, future-focused learning. Networks like XQ America, Deeper Learning, Big Picture Learning, iNacol, Next Gen Learning, Education Reimagined, and Transcend Learning have grown, linked school leaders, funded dozens of innovative school design teams, and are attracting new member schools every month. Free EdCamps and education Twitter chats that did not exist a decade ago are attended by tens of thousands of educators each year. Many professional learning providers offer virtual courses and meet-ups so they can share what is working with educators who can't afford the time and money to attend expensive conferences. Individual schools and districts create their own free and inexpensive design and meet-up days so the local change agents can share what works, not in theory, but in very real, practical ways.

The big point here is that *none of us have to reinvent the wheel alone* in order to build value in our schools. We have passed a fundamental tipping point in the evolution of human connectivity. For millennia, big ideas spread through a highly constricted pipeline. Masses of humanity listened to a handful of political, religious, or social influencers and followed where those few led. Humans were a metaphorical crowd of 10,000 people listening for one good idea from each of 10 people. Today, we are a metaphorical and very real crowd of 10,000 people sharing 10,000 good ideas. The power of this is staggering.

As individual change leaders, schools, and districts dive into the value–strategy–innovation discussion and as they start to listen to their stakeholders, we see convergence around the problems, the opportunities, the solutions, and how school communities start to make changes that will build value. This does *not* mean that all schools will look the same; that is exactly *opposite* of what is happening in the K–12 marketplace. People are different, and the kind of learning they seek for their children is therefore different. We are not looking for the one-size-fits-all secret sauce that you can pour on your school. But we are seeing convergence around *how* learning will better serve students and *how* schools can change as quickly and sustainably as possible.

The Three Horizons

The first description I could find of what we now call the Three Horizons Model was by Baghai, Coley, and White in their 1999 book *The Alchemy of Growth*. It's a simple tool, but one that should be a part of any school's strategic ethos because true innovation, the kind that can shift a school from "possibly irrelevant" to "potentially irreplaceable," rarely lies within the horizon we can see or on the ground right in front of us.

Horizon 1 is life as we know it. It contains the daily routines, programs, business, schedules, curricula, and people of school as it has been done for many decades. Horizon 1 keeps educators busy—so busy, in fact, that for most of us it seems impossible to free our vision and bandwidth to look beyond those daily stressors. It is tough to tear our attention away from the immediate needs of our students and teachers. Making changes within Horizon 1 involves tweaking what we already do each day: trying a new unit in an existing class, changing textbooks, making a minor change to the daily schedule or routine. A Horizon 1 change is "We need a new textbook," "Let's shift to Singapore math," or "Let's update our advisory program."

Horizon 2 is life as it is evolving in real time. We see and recognize that the world around our schools is changing due to technology, communication, demographics, marketplaces, and the nature of our students who are not, in many ways, the same as those of previous generations. As noted by the International Futures Forum, "Business as usual begins to feel out of place or no longer fit for our purpose." When we elevate our collective vision to Horizon 2, we embrace the freedom to significantly adjust, or even eliminate, one or more elements of the school operating system: a schoolwide commitment to project-based or design-based learning; a dramatic change in uses of time and space; introduction of interdisciplinary courses; smearing age and grade-level boundaries. A Horizon 2 change is "Let's merge our math and science departments and offer longer blocks of time so students can engage in interdisciplinary projects that may result in real-world impacts."

Horizon 3 is life in the unknown. It represents a completely different way of doing things. We don't know what "school" might be when we look toward Horizon 3, but we know, based on everything we see around us in a rapidly changing world, that it *does* exist. It is where the real disruptions lie, those that could push our own school into the dustbin alongside Betamax tapes, floppy disks, Walkmans, Blockbuster Video, landlines, and (potentially) shopping malls, taxis, gas stations, snail mail,

TV networks, and print journalism. Horizon 3 contains what education might be in a future that is still fuzzy but is almost certain to evolve over the next 10 to 20 years. Making changes within Horizon 3 requires that we throw out the existing playbook and start with a blank piece of paper: learning with and from people who are not present in our physical building; discarding the physical building altogether; 24/7/365 learning options; student–teacher co-learner cohorts. A Horizon 3 change might be "Let's turn our campus into a daily meeting center with health and social supports and sufficient bandwidth that our students can strap on the VR and learn face-to-face with teachers and other students anywhere in the world."

Educators have to decide what horizon they are focusing on. On a daily basis, you focus on Horizon 1 because that is your job; your students need you to provide a safe, effective learning environment.

In the midterm, you focus on Horizon 2 because you realize that much of the traditional school model does not result in the best learning that you can offer today.

To thrive sustainably in the long term, to ensure that families continue to choose your school, you have to seek out and focus on Horizon 3, a place of understanding value, creating strategies, and jump-starting innovations, even when you don't know where they might lead. You and your community come to see Horizon 3 as a place of "necessary survival."

There is no recipe for what mix of horizons your school needs to consider, but it is likely that long-term success will require all three.

Five Big, Hairy Challenges

Some educators are in it for the paycheck; most are in it because we believe we can help to positively influence rising generations. That majority is playing the long game. Yes, we are burdened every day by those commitments in Horizon 1 that take our attention, but we have a natural affinity for Horizon 3 as well. We aspire to have long-term positive impact.

For several years, I have been talking about some of the "big, hairy challenges" facing educators who want to have real, positive impact on both our students and on the world writ large (see Figure 19.1). These challenges rise to the top of a list like this because if we don't get *these* right, the rest just won't matter. My list may well not be yours; there may be overlap, or there may be none, and I celebrate both. Mine have been strongly influenced by what I see, who I have observed, and what I read, as will yours. I share mine not so you and your teams will come on board with them, but so you will perhaps find a bit more time to think in these dimensions and likewise share what you think is, or should be, dominating the top third of our collective race-car windshield.

How do those five challenges fit into this book, and why do I share them here at the end? Because I am utterly convinced that any school that incorporates these into practice, that begins to deliver on solutions to these challenges, will have a differentiated value proposition that will set it apart from all others for many years to come.

Figure 19.1 Five Big, Hairy Challenges for Schools

1. **First** is the ability and willingness to engage in civil discourse. Democracy is a foundational hope for human society, and the designers of democracy, including the Great American Experiment, assumed civil discourse as a way of solving problems. Our current generation of leaders is in the process of destroying this profound foundation. Polarization of thought and the inability to compromise nurture fanaticism. The center may not hold. As educators, we simply must train ourselves and our students in the skills and responsibilities of civil discourse.

2. **Second** is the ability and commitment to separate fact from fiction. To me, the most profound inflection point in the history of humanity was the rise of the rule of law, which requires that we collectively hold certain things to be true, not subject to the whim of those with the most power. Recent studies out of MIT prove that *falsity travels six times faster on Twitter* than does truth. It is profoundly dangerous that many Americans are willing to sacrifice the truth to their own selfish points of view. Dictators do this, and we are supposed to be better.

3. **Third** is respect for expertise. With the rise of social media, anyone who can gather an online following can sway public opinion. As many as 50 percent of Americans accept the opinions of *self-proclaimed* experts over those by people with a lifetime of expertise behind them. It sounds politically incorrect, but *not all opinions have equal value*. We have to help students figure out how to give more weight to those who have earned it.

4. **Fourth** is empathy. In a flatter, closer, more interrelated world, if we cannot see through the eyes and experiences of those who look and live differently than we do, our version of society is doomed to the same dustbin of history as the monarchical, communist, and fascist experiments of the last thousand years.

5. **Fifth** is technology. As futurist Gerd Leonhard (2016) explains, modern technologies like the iPhone go through a magic phase where we wonder at their power; a manic phase where we cannot do without them; and a toxic phase where they start to take over our lives. For 20 years, we educators have been pushing Internet connectivity as the greatest learning tool in the history of humankind, which it is, only to now see just how toxic, stressful, and damaging overconnectivity can become (Twenge, 2017). We need to find the right balance for ourselves and our students between a headlong rush to be the most wired, best-coding, STEM factories that will crank out workers for the post-information age and what Leonhard (2016) describes as the human buffer against a tech-ruled world: places of "CORE" where we give equal weight to that which we reserve for our humanness: compassion, originality, responsibility, and empathy.

Reflect

In the introduction, I set out a road map for these chapters, and I want to wrap up with an opportunity for you to reflect and synthesize. It would be warmly gratifying to end with a single, simple grand unified theory or a formula like $E = mc^2$ into which you can plug a few key variables and find

Figure 19.2 Metaphors Guiding This Book

North Star	A *common aiming point* for the organization; a framework around which to align vision, systems, and daily work
The Tree	A *framework* that links the key ideas of value, strategy, and innovation
The Tool Belt	A *set of processes* that can be used to move the school from where it is to where you want it to be
Stairway	A *checklist* of key organizational elements that are needed to achieve successful innovation
The Architect	A *leadership archetype* that is best suited to an organization that wants to embrace distributed leadership and design-based problem solving
Horizons	A *rubric* for testing where your own and your school's focus lies

your school's perfect path. But that is not the case, or at least I have not found that unified formula yet. The process of identifying and doing the work of school transformation is not simple, but I have suggested a number of processes, frameworks, and tools that can be used at different points along your path. The metaphors for each are also not unified; they are also not interchangeable, and each is useful in its own way. Like the initial road map, then, Figure 19.2 presents a summary of images and metaphors that, I argue, are not mixed at all, but each appropriate to its own context.

It is also inviting, at this point, to want a rubric against which you can evaluate your school—to tell you what to do and when—that will spit out a grade for where your school lies on the continuum between failing and thriving now and in the future. It is inviting, but not real. These chapters have contained a variety of organizational, cultural, procedural, intellectual, and relational skills and processes, each of which comes with its own set of key questions and each of which must be "graded" differently. If there is one template that is truly flexible enough to work for all schools, granular enough to capture the rigor that these processes demand, and still honors the complexity of the problem, I have not discovered it yet. I urge you to develop a set of essential questions and measurements appropriate to *your* school; working the problem in this way is a key to building transformational muscle in your school. If you find that grand rubric, share it!

Go

Peter Drucker famously said, "Culture eats strategy for breakfast." As a response, a really insightful teacher asked me, "But what if our school doesn't have a change-focused culture? Don't we need a strategy to create one?" I was shockingly disappointed that I, and many others, had missed this Zen-like pitfall embedded in Drucker's dictum.

Ultimately, change at schools is a chicken-and-egg process. We have to create a culture that embraces change in theory and then build the muscles to implement change in sustainable practice. For many of us, a school that is ready to act on much of what you read in this book will have been a pipe dream. It is hard for you to see *your* school getting there any time soon. And yet, many schools just like yours with many of the same problems, obstacles, and challenges are embracing the challenges of sustainable change that will allow them to thrive in the future. They are thinking, planning, interacting, and working differently from you.

How do you know if your school is really ready? How do you build confidence that any of this is actually working? Tipping points are those moments in time, process, or emotional commitment when an individual or organization is probably not going to slide backward. What might some of those tipping points look like for schools? When can people start to redirect the fear of failure to the optimism of likely success?

Figure 19.3 has some examples of what these tipping points might be.

What will be the tipping point for your school or district? What might be the next steps you can take to create the best conditions for a long future

Figure 19.3 What Will Tip You Toward Innovation?

- When a school community collectively decides that it is going to create and sustain a culture that embraces change.
- When your team realizes you can lose the future if you forget the past, but you can't win the future with the past as your guide.
- When the community of a school sees the rapidly changing world as an incredible opportunity rather than an insurmountable problem.
- When school leaders with big titles stop leading for others and create the conditions that allow others to lead for themselves.
- When a school community realizes that the risk of not changing is less than the risk of changing.
- When many adults in the school decide that
  - what they want to do as educators is a greater force than the fears that hold them back.
  - they want something different than what they have and are willing to make changes to achieve it.
  - the best way to get students to push outside their comfort zones is to model this for them.
  - they can't control everything, but they will own what they can control.
- Most educators are either willing or eager to try something new if they are given the resources to try and support if they fail.
- Our self-worth as educators is not defined by what we know but by our willingness to strive to learn.
- When you come to the conclusion that the tailwinds that support you to move forward are actually much more impactful than are the headwinds that hold you back.
- Your school team has the courage to subtract things they do today in order to make room for things they want to do tomorrow.

of *thriving* in your school? How can you create excitement about becoming the school that is irresistible to your customers?

These are the questions you want to pose with those around you. This is the conversation that will determine future success in an uncertain world. I really want *all* schools to survive this period of evolution, but they won't—and what I want does not matter. What *you* want does.

Keep Going

As I said in the introduction, the process of value-enriching evolution in a time of rapid external changes is not something that starts and stops. There is no one point where you take a tool out of the strategic design tool kit, use it, and then replace it to gather dust for a few years.

When I hiked for a month in the Himalayas many years ago, up and down and up and down each day on seemingly endless sets of steps carved out of the cliff sides, gaining elevation each day into thinning air, the only way to finish each long ascent was to *not* stop, to set a doable pace and just keep going. If I stopped or sat down to rest, each restart was harder than the last. Dealing with VUCA world demands that you set a pace for your school and keep going. There is no end to being great and in demand. It is your new organizational state of being. Pull out the tools you need when you need them. Sometimes, you might conclude that a certain activity was a failure. Fine. It happens. Learn from it. The only real failure will be if you use that as a reason to stop the process rather than learning from it and carrying on.

Gather. Share. Listen. "Do. Or do not. There is no try," said Master Yoda. Forgive me, but in this (one and only?) case, Master Yoda is wrong.

Try. Keep trying . . . frequently. Iterate often. Build. Keep listening, even when you think you know the answers your students and families will give you. Listen to what your families want, not just what they say they need. Make tough choices. Fearlessly let go of what is no longer yielding top value for your families. Carve out a niche where you are offering what no one else can offer as well as you can and ferociously defend it. Become what your families would give up last.

> Try. Keep trying . . . frequently. Iterate often. Build. Keep listening, even when you think you know the answers.

If your school is the one doing these, you *will* not only survive, but "thrive" the revolution!

Appendix I

Activities for Your Teams

For the last seven years, I have had the privilege of working with diverse groups of school community stakeholders in a wide variety of settings: conference workshops, single-school or districtwide professional development days, longer projects to develop and implement strategic visions, and, perhaps my favorite, spending time with students.

My own work and that of an increasing number of other educators have several elements in common that lead to more powerful, long-lasting impacts with school teams (see Figure A).

Many of these activities I have made up on my own, though I certainly borrowed elements from other sources as I have moved along my own trajectory. Others, as noted, I have stolen from or co-created with colleagues; we all believe in sharing with attribution. If I have failed to remember the origin of any of these, I apologize. Many of these activities are "design-based," meaning they have their roots in or intersect with design-thinking protocols that are becoming increasingly adopted in schools as well as in noneducation organizations. I invite you to use and modify these and then reshare the results!

The activities in this appendix are in four groups:

- Activities Most Closely Related to Section I (Chapters 1–5)

- Activities Most Closely Related to Section II (Chapters 6–10)

Figure A Tips for More Powerful School Team Activities

- **Diversity matters.** We simply must get beyond the normal silos that artificially separate us in our work. Thought provoking—and, in some cases, groundbreaking—workshops often include teachers, administrators, trustees, students, alumni, and parents in the same room.

- **Many activities work at any scale.** I have conducted many of these activities with groups ranging from 12 to 250 participants. In almost every case, the more the better. Larger groups create infectious energy, and people see firsthand that they are not alone in their hopes, dreams, ideas, and concerns.

- **Make results transparent.** Unless there is some compelling reason to the contrary, results can be tabulated and shared in order to prompt feedback and further discussion from both those who attend and those who do not.

- **Be noisy.** Noise is the sound of great learning.

- **Create visible learning.** We paper walls, windows, and any other vertical surface with butcher paper, flip chart paper, and sticky-note collages that provide very tangible evidence of shared learning.

- **Small working or breakout groups are most effective.** Their optimal size ranges from five to eight people. If there are any fewer, you don't have a diverse and creative stew; any more, and some people will not be engaged.

- **Be creative.** We use *a lot* of sticky notes and colorful marker pens!

- Activities Most Closely Related to Section III (Chapters 11–19)
- Activities Useful in Any Setting

A Note on Notes

Sticky notes may be our single most powerful tool for "unwrapping" the thinking of a group of people. Sticky notes are powerful for four reasons. *First*, they allow anonymity. We know from numerous studies that in any group once one person voices an opinion, the chance of anyone voicing an opposing opinion drops dramatically. *Second*, they require brevity. I usually ask that each sticky note contain one word, phrase, or sentence. This allows the notes to be gathered and entered into a sortable format for future synthesis. *Third*, as opposed to 3-by-5 cards, or even a shared digital pin board, sticky notes can be easily rearranged, so your work is dynamic, not static. *Fourth*, posting up on walls and windows makes group ideas visible and usable for other activities, and it allows for ideas to be moved closer to each other and grouped together.

I recommend having sticky notes on hand almost any time a group gathers, including students in the classroom. Creative teachers find that using sticky notes allows students who are less likely to raise their hand to contribute more and keeps many students engaged rather than having only one student answer at a time.

A Note on Students and Titles

Some of the activities in this appendix are adults only, but not as many as you might think. We have vastly underestimated and underleveraged the input of students when it comes to rethinking the learning experience. There is definitely a lesser return with younger students, but every time I have convinced adults to let high school students participate in many of these activities, the takeaway is universally "Why haven't we done this before?" As you look at these activities, I strongly urge you to ask, "Why would we *not* want student voice in the room?"

Having students in the room also reminds us that, for many if not all of these activities, it is best that everyone enters the room as equals; leave your titular hats at the door. Those with lofty titles who participate must work to not be the center of attention; those with less lofty titles must work to lead with strong voices.

Activities That Align With Section I: The Road to "Thrive": Strategy, Value, Innovation

Activity I.1

Covey Quadrants (30 minutes)

Purpose: Prioritizing use of time and other resources

In almost every school, the urgent gets in the way of the important. If we make that the default, the problem never gets better. In 2004, Stephen Covey published the simple model that has become known as Covey Quadrants (see Figure B), and having your team fill it out is a quick way to get beyond the frustrations that the "important" is always crowded out of your lives.

Figure B Covey Quadrants

	URGENT	NOT URGENT
IMPORTANT		"QUADRANT OF QUALITY"
NOT IMPORTANT		

We know that in schools we have to attend to what is both urgent and important. We also know we spend too much time on things that *appear* urgent in the moment but are not important with a longer perspective. And we know the "not urgent and not important" clutter *really* needs to be either cleared out or ignored.

What jumps out in the Covey model is that *creative quality is most often found in the top-right corner, and we have to make time for it.* Innovation is extremely important, but we think of it as less urgent than the things that keep us awake at night and busy all day. If you want your school to change in ways that will grow value, you simply must create time and space for working in the top-right Covey Quadrant. Effectively innovative schools build sacred time into daily and weekly schedules for the upper-right quadrant.

Bring this tool out once a quarter or so for updating by an admin team. See if people agree with what lies in each quadrant. If not, discuss!

Activity I.2

Four Futures Map (40–60 minutes)

Purpose: Increasing and expanding long-range vision

I borrowed this crystal-ball exercise from the Institute for the Future, a Palo Alto–based think tank that helps industries ranging from health care to high tech and education to plan more strategically for the less-predictable future.

Each table team divides a piece of flip chart paper or an area on a whiteboard into four quadrants. In each quadrant, they "sketch" a very different possible future for the organization (e.g., department, school, district) at a point in the future, usually 10 or 20 years. I encourage teams to actually draw pictures rather than relying on more comfortable bullet points. I always suggest that one of the quadrants represent an "apocalyptic" future, one in which the organization has ceased to exist or be relevant.

Then, for each possible future, the teams create a list of indicators—"canaries in the coal mine"—that would occur or be evident as the respective future is evolving. What signs would we see as this future evolves?

Finally, each team, or a sampling of teams, shares at least one future with the entire group, usually the future that they think other teams might not have created.

Four Futures is most effective alongside other activities like Headline Writing, Post-It Questions, and Jobs to Be Done—ones that generate a large repository of visible ideas about the future. If some of the potential futures are *not* pretty wild and out of the school's current comfort zone, encourage teams to press their thinking harder. It is almost certain that (within the next 10 to 20 years) challenges to the school status quo will come from other learning experiences that we are *not* thinking about today.

Activity I.3

Headline Writing (20–40 minutes)

Purpose: Finding all-school aspirations

I stole this activity from Bo Adams, who likely borrowed it from someone else. Like the Four Futures activity, it helps teams look to the future but this time with the added benefit of uncovering their own biggest aspirations. This is a critical activity for North Star development; it asks us to think of "our best selves; our best school" without regard to the constraints and limitations that usually strangle truly aspirational thinking.

The prompt is simple: *At a point in the future (usually 10 or 20 years), a major national news show such as* 60 Minutes *is coming to your school to do a story. Why would they do that? What is happening or has happened here that warrants such powerful attention?*

Each person writes a headline for that hypothetical story. It is critical that people are able to think about this future story without being bound by "reality"—the headlines can be almost mythical if they want! (You will find that, even given this freedom, many people will write headlines that are clearly *not* worthy of national attention; this is a sign of just how constrained many of us are in our thinking of what is possible in schools. Give some collegial feedback when you see this; remind those participants of the freedom inherent in this activity and ask them to try again.)

Depending on the number of people and time available, there are several ways to continue once each person has written a headline.

Option 1: Write the headline on a piece of paper. Pass that paper to the person to the right or left at the table. Each recipient then writes the start of a short "lead" for the article that would attend the headline they have received. After a few minutes, the paper is passed again to the right, and the next person adds to the growing article under a headline that he or she did not write. This way, the team sees what others are thinking, and a story evolves for each headline idea.

Option 2: Write all of the headlines from each table team on a piece of flip chart paper. Then, post all of the flip chart papers full of headlines around the room. Then all group members walk and read the headlines and give "approval votes" for the ones they like best using sticky dots or just making dots using marker pens. (In approval voting, I usually like to give each person the right to vote for 5 percent to 20 percent of the total options available. So if there are 50 headlines around the room, each person might get to place between three and 10 dots.) Using approval voting, you will see which of the aspirational futures are most exciting to the entire group.

Activity 1.4

Gathering Data for a North Star (3–10 minutes)

Purpose: Building a dataset around aspirations

Any time a group of your stakeholders gathers is an opportunity to collect information on their thinking. Using sticky notes, you can gather feedback to multiple prompts in just a few minutes. Some of the questions/prompts I have found most valuable in the North Star phase of strategic design are as follows:

> What does great teaching look like to you?
>
> What are some indicators of great learning?
>
> What hopes and dreams do you have for our students/children?
>
> Write questions that start with "What if . . ." (one question per sticky note) that would change something at the school in a way that you think would be really beneficial.

Once a team has generated a lot of sticky notes, they should sort them into groups or themes and *name the group*. In this way, the team is seeing and working with their thinking in real time. Also make sure to collect the sticky notes and get them typed into lists; they are powerful artifacts of the group's collective thinking and can be turned into word clouds or studied further. The goal of this work, as shown in Figure C, is realized in three stages: *gathering* raw data, *finding* the big themes, and *distilling* top targets for your North Star.

To gather this kind of information from community stakeholders who are *not* at school every day (parents, other caregivers), consider having a school-wide or districtwide No Homework Day. At one small district I worked with, the students all took home a single piece of paper made to look like four sticky notes, each with one of the questions bulleted earlier. Their only homework that evening was to get a parent or other adult in the home to fill it out with words or short phrases and return it the next day (no names attached). We had more than 70 percent returned, which is unheard of in a regular e-mail survey!

Activity 1.5

Tradition and Innovation (20–40 minutes)

Purpose: Finding balance between old and new

Schools that have been successful in the past can easily get stuck on the questions of "What do we keep?" and "What can we change?" Many schools

Figure C Organizing Data to Find Your North Star

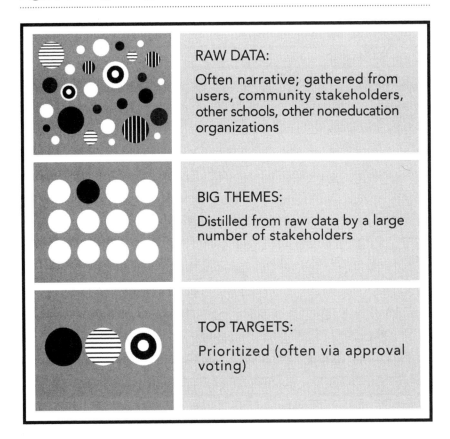

RAW DATA:

Often narrative; gathered from users, community stakeholders, other schools, other noneducation organizations

BIG THEMES:

Distilled from raw data by a large number of stakeholders

TOP TARGETS:

Prioritized (often via approval voting)

have traditions and practices that are core to their value proposition, and many stakeholders are fearful that innovation means changing these important, often emotionally precious traditions.

On a flip chart paper or section of a whiteboard, table teams set up two columns: *Things We Should Never Change* and *Things We Can Change*; using sticky notes, brainstorm, post, and discuss the results of the two columns. Generally, I find that after some discussion, some of the items in the *Never Change* column get moved to the *We Can Change* column. At a minimum, there is great discussion about often-emotional attachments we all have to our traditions.

Activity I.6

Future Frame—Building a New Web Page (60–90 minutes)

Purpose: Putting flesh on the bones of an aspirational idea

This activity comes from the Mt. Vernon Institute for Innovation (MVIFI) at Mt. Vernon Presbyterian School, a must-follow if your school wants to know how to use design-based routines for creating value-rich innovation. As with the Headline Writing activity, this protocol allows small teams to look into the future and use the creative side of their brains to sketch what that future might actually look like.

Figure D "Future Frame" Template

Using the template in Figure D, teams build a website landing page for a possible pilot project or program that they are imagining or prototyping (see Figure D).

For this activity, teams should be grouped into either two or three people; any more, and someone is not going to be fully engaged and sketching. The key elements of this template are as follows:

- Http line: What is the name of the pilot or program?

- Menu: What would be the key subpages that people would want to find?

- Slider: Draw some images that would flow across the page to excite the reader.

- Services: What are some key elements of the pilot project? Use sketches and words.

- Recent Posts: What are some headlines and at least one image of a blog about the project that would attract attention?

Emphasize this: No one wants to read a bunch of bullet lists on a web page! Provocative sketches and pictures both encourage creative thinking and will attract more attention and discussion from users.

Once the time is up (I suggest about 45 minutes for the design phase), hang the templates around the room for all to see. One member of each team might stay next to their poster to answer questions. Hand out dots for approval voting for the "best" or most interesting or provocative Future Frames. Take pictures of all of them to share with trustees or parents as an example of your group creative thinking.

Activities That Align With Section II: The Five Big Tools of Strategic Change for Schools

Activity II.1

Six Circles (10 minutes) or Three Circles (6 minutes)

Purpose: Jump-starting creativity

Also from the design laboratory of MVIFI and their former colleague Mary Cantwell, this is another activity that stimulates the creative right side of the brain. It can be done either as six circles in 10 minutes or three circles in 6 minutes.

I usually use this activity right after a Gallery Walk and before starting a group prototyping activity. It is remarkable how it can quickly bring out key ideas that were imprinted on each person in the short Gallery Walk. Each person takes a piece of paper and draws six (or three) big open circles. Then, with the clock running, they have an equal number of minutes to draw sketches of possible ideas or outcomes to a challenge question. The only rules are that the sketches have to be different from each other, and they cannot contain *any* words or numbers; these are pure drawings.

At the end of the sketching period, the table team selects a timekeeper, and each person has no more than one minute to share/explain all of her or his sketches to the rest of the team. This is a fabulous way to unlock creative thinking and to rapidly share with others what is sitting uppermost in each person's mind before the team launches into rapid prototyping of solutions.

Activity II.2

Building a Road Map (1–4 hours, or more)

Purpose: Aligning big moves across the school

Once a school or team has validated the need to make a significant change, building a plan of how to make it happen is critical. If you are following the

Logic Model, this is part of the Activities section and not before! A "road map" can be simple or complex, depending on the magnitude of the change and how many people and groups are impacted. The most complex problems require a dedicated project manager, and in some cases, they can even benefit from the use of program management software that guides the manager in creating a "critical path" of activities, resources, and deadlines.

But for most school projects, manual road maps using the following steps are highly effective:

- Use a large blank wall or a long piece of butcher paper rolled out on tables in the conference room or cafeteria. Don't scrimp on space—a team of six to eight road map designers will feel less cramped if they have 15 to 25 linear feet of space to work with.

- Use sticky notes; it is easier to move them around than to constantly erase and rewrite.

- On the horizontal axis, create a timeline; for big projects, you might want to map out the next year in months and subsequent years in quarters.

- On the vertical axis, put the major themes or areas of the school that will be impacted; these might include schedule, teaching assignments, admissions cycle, classroom renovations, curriculum and materials development, professional training, and so on.

- Start filling in the road map with activities that are needed in sequence. I prefer starting at the end of a big block of time, such as a school year; decide what you need to deliver at specific points and work backward from those hard deadlines.

- Once the team has a draft road map, take pictures of it or leave it on the wall if you can, so it can be updated in real time. School road maps are like military battles: No plan of attack lasts longer than the first engagement with the "enemy"!

Activity II.3

School Research (20–60 minute blocks)

Purpose: Not reinventing the wheel!

Perhaps the most powerful innovation advantage that education has over nearly every other industry is that we love to freely share, steal, and borrow from each other. While physically visiting colleagues at other schools is always a great idea, the time, distance, and budget constraints often limit the ability of educators to visit other schools and classrooms in person.

That limitation is becoming less of an obstacle every day. With video chat capability, we can not only talk face-to-face with almost anyone anywhere, but we can also share pictures, videos, files, syllabi—pretty much anything—during a video chat. For no charge, we can meet one-on-one or in groups of up to 40 or 50 on platforms such as Skype, Google Hangout, Face Time, and Zoom.

Even fast, simple web searches yield troves of information about a school, as many teachers and students are now posting student projects, videos from their classrooms, syllabi, blog posts, and detailed information about pilots and programs that they think are helping to "lead" their school.

A great activity for a faculty meeting looks something like this, but you can create all kinds of variations:

- Preselect one topic or theme or have attendees choose topics or themes that align with your aspirational vision of learning at your school. If you have developed a North Star, these themes should be highly visible in that document.

- Seed the activity with schools or people who we know are already working in this area. If you don't have even a starter list, team members can start searching on Google or with Edutopia, which is the best site I know to search for who and where innovative learning is taking root. Appendix II has a long list of schools and other resources that will also likely contain leads for some of the themes to which you are attracted.

- Each team member visits two or three school websites or the websites of two or three education practitioners who are working in the area of interest. They take notes and look for links to people, programs, resources, networks, and other schools to quickly expand the range of further searches.

- Start a Google Doc or page on your shared school platform so team members can post links that warrant further research or a personal contact.

- After the teams have collected a list of schools or people who might have valuable knowledge to share, set a goal for team members to contact *someone* beyond your school via e-mail and hold at least one video chat with at least one person at one other school, posting the interview results on the shared Google Doc.

Within a very short period of time, you can acquire a huge trove of ideas about learning options that other schools have already tested and refined. Your teams will become comfortable with reaching out to colleagues and schools to access the wealth of shared knowledge that is within a few keystrokes. You will be well on your way to developing a school culture that values connectivity, not isolation . . . and all for the lowest possible cost in time and money.

Activity II.4

Risk-Taking (10 minutes)

Purpose: Assessing comfort with taking risks

Is your school team willing or eager to try new things? Are they listening to repeated pleas that it is OK to take a risk in their teaching practice? Ask them! In this simple, quick activity, your team can measure their collective feelings about risk-taking and also identify where their individual feelings fall with respect to the larger group.

First, draw three big number lines from 1 to 10 on a whiteboard or length of butcher paper.

Then, for each of the following questions, individuals will write a number from 1 to 10 on a scrap of paper or sticky note. For each prompt, *1* represents "not at all," while *10* represents "big time!" Ask the questions one at a time before revealing the next question:

- On a scale of 1 to 10, how *eager* are you to take risks and try new things in your teaching practice?

- On a scale of 1 to 10, how *willing* are you to try new things in your teaching practice?

- On a scale of 1 to 10, how much do you think your (principal, superintendent, division leader) *wants* you to try new things?

For each question, allow about 10 seconds for the numbers to be written; then, have a small group of people collect all of the notes and create stacked dots on each of the three respective number lines, which will look something like the graph in Figure E.

Every school where I have done this activity responds with a surprisingly "risk-willing" distribution. Those who tend to be willing to try new things see that they are supported by many colleagues. Those who are not willing see that they are outliers and feel more empowered to join the

Figure E   How Risk-Willing Are You?

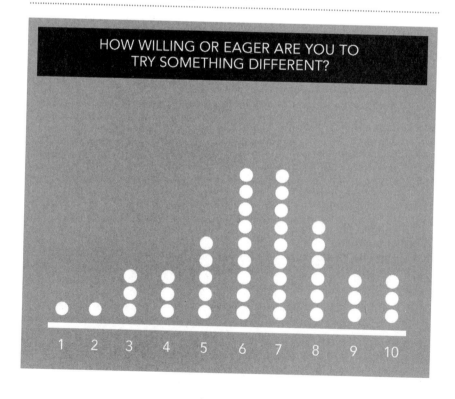

risk-takers. And since this quick survey is anonymous, school leaders can gauge if their message of wanting teachers to try new things is actually getting across.

Activities That Align With Section III: Start Building

Activity III.1

Creating a Great North Star (a few hours to a few months)

Purpose: Defining all-school aiming points

Here is a more detailed outline of the activities you can conduct in the process of creating a North Star. These work at all scales, whether your North Star project is for a grade level, department, school, or district. It is important to limit the time frame in which to create a North Star, or this can go on for many months, which usually means the group really does not want to make critical choices.

Unwrap

Ask open-ended questions rather than give surveys that allow relatively few and narrow ranges of answers. Most importantly, ask questions that provoke open-ended thinking, not simplistic answers. Use sticky notes because they are anonymous and the writer is limited to a very few words:

- What does great learning look like to you?
- What does great teaching look like to you?
- What hopes and dreams do you have for your students/children?
- What one word would you hope that people would use to describe your school?
- How is the school serving the needs of its students, and why?
- How might the school do a better job of serving the needs of all students?
- Why did you decide to become a member of this school community as opposed to other choices you had?

And perhaps the most powerful of all . . .

- Write questions on sticky notes that start with the words *what if*—that most powerful question—because uniquely *unlike* her sister queries that start with *who*, *what*, *where*, and *when*, there is no absolute answer to a what-if question. By its very nature, these questions lead us into areas of potential creativity.

Paper the walls with posters and sticky notes, with sketches, musings, headlines, word groupings, and bullet lists. Not everyone will agree with all that is on the walls—that is not the goal of unwrapping. But as you share and study what the group has imagined, you will see that there are more areas of agreement than disagreement and that your community shares a number of fundamental aspirations that overlap with the best nature of great learning. Team members see that they are part of a community that *wants* to make changes if they can only see *how* we collectively can make it all work. Find those big points of overlap.

Listen

Discovery involves finding times and opportunities to engage a wide group of users in the discussion of what they value. Rather than wasting Back to School Night handing out syllabi that could be e-mailed or carried home, turn these precious face-to-face opportunities with parents into discovery and listening events. Hold a schoolwide or districtwide No Homework Day as I described earlier. At the start of faculty meetings, have teachers generate sticky notes for three minutes around an "unwrapping" question or give feedback on a new pilot or idea for the school.

Using these simple, fast, anonymous, inclusive methods, you can gather a very large volume of data about what the extended school community actually thinks and believes. As these ideas are distilled into a North Star, your stakeholders see themselves *in* the process of designing innovative change, not recipients of change foisted *upon* them.

Filter

One word or short phrase answers can be typed into a spreadsheet. Even a bad typist like me can enter more than 100 sticky note responses in an hour. Spread the work around, and a team can log all of these data into a shared spreadsheet in no time. Then generate simple word clouds. With these two easy steps, we quickly see major trends begin to emerge.

Longer responses take a bit more distillation. If you end up with many hundreds of data points through all of the Unwrapping and Listening, have small teams of two or three people review a couple of hundred responses, sorting them into self-created "buckets" or themes. A team can review and distill 100 to 200 short answer responses in less than an hour. Then, the smaller working groups share their themes together to come up with a master list of the big, compelling themes that arise out of all of the data you have gathered.

Narrow

Analyze the many creative ideas and big themes that arise from your stakeholders and apply the filter of the strategy–value–innovation equation:

- Will it enhance the long-term value of the school?

- Will it differentiate our school/district in the eyes of customers?

- Does it align with our understanding of how students learn best?

- Will it help us "win" the inevitable race to attract students?

- Will it support systemwide creation, management, and measurement of value-building innovation?

- Is it truly aspirational? Will others get excited and rally to this flag? Does it reflect our best understanding of great learning?

By the end of this step, you will have a list of big themes and creative ideas that represent the aspirations of your community, and that can lead to the creation and implementation of a strong, differentiated value proposition.

Write

I strongly suggest that one person write a first draft of your North Star. An opening paragraph might give the overall vision of a powerful, differentiated value proposition centered on what great learning looks like at the school or how that value stands apart in the local marketplace. Subsequent paragraphs articulate the big themes that rose to the top of this North Star process.

How many themes should be included? There is no hard answer for that, but I would suggest that for most schools, any more than six or seven begins to look like an unwillingness or inability to ask the difficult questions in the filtering process.

A very small committee should help revise the first draft. Challenge each other on achieving brevity and specificity. Toss out the platitudes that always find their way into documents such as this. Write what you really mean in ways that others will understand. Try to capture the passions and excitement of those first Unwrapping activities *before* people started to worry how *actually* doing those things might impact their own practice and lives!

Open the revised first draft for discussion and comments, along with all of the data from the Unwrapping activities. Gather feedback from as many stakeholders as possible. Did we capture the big themes? Did we miss something important? Is the wording clear?

Finalize the document. The goal is not to make everyone happy with every word. I like to say that a great working North Star that will serve an evolving community is one in which 80 percent of the people agree with 80 percent of the document. When it is in final form, how will it be validated? Is this something that needs to go to the principal, the superintendent, or the board for formal approval? If so, then get that done. Without formal acceptance, the North Star can be waived off by naysayers who are threatened by the changes it contains, in which case the entire process will have been largely a waste of time.

Activity III.2

Culture of Teaching/Culture of Learning (40 minutes)

Purpose: Shifting group mindset

As we discussed in Chapter 13, the fundamental shift in schools as we evolve away from the Industrial Age model is that we are becoming focused on *learning*, not *teaching*. What does this actually mean? How do these cultures look different in practice? What will that shift mean for your school, your teachers, and your students? How does a culture of adult learning influence student learning, and how does that culture manifest in a school? (You may want to preface this activity by a group read over the summer of one or more of the books that I cited in the chapter.)

First, table teams brainstorm the characteristics of a "learning organization" (remember that this applies to both adults and students!). How do teachers approach their responsibilities and their relationships with students differently? What might this look like from the student perspective?

Then, using approval voting, each table team highlights three to five characteristics that are most impactful across all grade levels.

Finally, table groups share their highlights, and the larger group (either in real time or at a next meeting) crafts an overall set of guiding lights for what it means to be a school that is focused on learning. Administrators can then use this list to develop a professional growth plan to help both adults and students to develop these skills and tactics.

Activity III.3

What We Can/Can't Control (15–45 minutes)

Purpose: Empowering change agents; declawing myths

One of the most common and stubborn obstacles to enacting change is the sense that we are trapped by conditions beyond our control. The mythology around what professional educators or student learners can and cannot control can kill an innovation culture before it has a chance to be born. There are real obstacles to change that *are* beyond our control: overused standardized testing, seat time regulations, rigid subject requirements, outdated required textbooks, and the like.

But we *can* control much of what seems difficult to control: parent conversations, daily schedules, professional growth and collaboration, course outlines, and a great deal of our pedagogy and curriculum.

The activity is simple: Split a piece of flip chart paper or a section of whiteboard into two columns, one labeled *Can Control* and the other *Can't Control*. Team members brainstorm sticky notes and place them on one side or the other. Then, teams wander and see what all of the other teams have posted. During this Gallery Walk, anyone in the room has an opportunity to move the notes from one column to the other. Then, after one round of movement, announce that anyone in the room who feels that he or she can move a note from the *Can't* side to the *Can* side is free to do so without that note being moved back to *Can't*.

As a group, look at the result. If there are senior decision makers in the room, have them comment. We often find that there are notes on the *Can't Control* that we *know*, after additional discussion, we *can* control: parent chatter in the parking lot, trust among teachers and administrators, permission to innovate. (In one summer institute where we used this activity, the head of the school had specifically and repeatedly given the faculty broad permission to try new ideas, to take initiative without asking permission, and promised to find resources to support their efforts. Yet even after going through all three steps of this simple activity, there were sticky notes on the *Can't Control* side for which the CEO had explicitly promised control to those in the room!) It is a perfect opportunity to reinforce this degree of permission and authority by visibly moving those sticky notes to the *Can Control* column.

Activity III.4

What Do We Really Believe? (20–60 minutes)

Purpose: Clarifying aiming points

Every school has (or should have) a set of guiding documents that guide their work. These might include some or all of the following:

- Mission statement

- Vision statement

- Profile of a graduate

- School philosophy

- Pillars of instruction

- Core values

- Introductions or overviews of a strategic plan or accreditation

- Agreements between faculty and administration or between students and teachers that help govern how they work together

I have found two profoundly important opportunities to engage with these documents, and the more "guiding documents" that a school has, the more impactful this activity can be.

- First, print a copy of each document for every team member. If there are many guiding documents, or if they are long, you will have to select just one or a few for each time you practice this activity.

- Next, team members *individually* parse the selected documents with a highlighter, marking key words and phrases that each person feels are at the core of each bullet point or paragraph. Ask them to be as laser-like as possible: What are those individual words or phrases that are the real hinge-points of the generally long, wordy sentences that often fill these documents?

- Next, have all team members (remember, a good working team is between five and eight people) list the words and phrases they have highlighted on some flip chart paper or whiteboard. There will be a lot of similar notes, so it helps to just go through the documents one sentence at a time, giving the team the chance to post up a word or phrase.

- Once the team has posted all of their key words and phrases, there are two activity opportunities, and both can be real eye-openers:

Option 1: Using approval voting, each team should *prioritize* the lists: Which of all of these words or phrases does each person think are the MOST important among what will be very long lists? (Again, in approval voting, I usually like to give each person the chance to vote using dots or marks for no more than 25 percent of the available options. In this case, when the lists might be quite long, you might want to limit it to just 5 percent to 10 percent). Once the dots are posted, circle the "winners" and then have multiple teams compare or make a master list. These represent what the entire group thinks are the most key points of what are often very long laundry lists of goals, objectives, or characteristics of the school. It forces us to be selective, which is more difficult than being completely inclusive.

Option 2: This option came to me one day when I was about to launch a group of faculty and administrators on Option 1. Once the list of words and phrases are collected by each working team, ask them to place *as many dots as they like* with a very specific instruction: Only place a dot next to a word or phrase *if you think that, in general, the school community knows what the word or phrase actually means.* These guiding documents are almost always chock full of platitudes and vague adjectives such as *great, excellent, generous, diverse,* and many more. In my experience, it is often the case that fewer than a quarter of the words *get any dots at all.* This stark realization forces the school community to get serious about actually defining who they are and what they want to be, rather than just creating lofty-sounding manifestos that don't actually mean anything.

Activity III.5

Impact Versus Difficulty (10–20 minutes)

Purpose: Prioritizing opportunities

Schools, like individuals and other organizations, can't do everything; we have to choose. One good way to look at a large number of ideas or opportunities is to create a simple scatter plot on which one axis is *Potential Impact* and the other is *Difficulty. Difficulty* can also be expressed as *Risk* or *Resource Outlay.* Teams place a dot or sticky note representing potential ideas or pilots where they think they belong on these two axes; sticky notes are better than marks because the team can discuss the placement and move the sticky note as they wish.

Then, the group analyzes the resulting scatter. Of course, we are always looking for new ideas that have the greatest potential impact for the least amount of difficulty or resources. But as with an investment portfolio, effective organizations want a good distribution of potential projects in the pipeline that represent an array of high-impact/high-risk and low-impact/lower-risk or difficulty.

Activity III.6

Map Your Market (1–2 hours)

Purpose: Knowing your customers

Many families at your school know at least some of their neighbors, and when friends of neighbors share good stories about their children's experiences at school, others listen. So for private and charter schools, and for districts with school choice, leaders can market their schools better if they know where their current families live and what might motivate others in those same neighborhoods to send their students to your school.

Basic customer mapping is easy. You can create a dot map by just importing family addresses into a free mapping tool. You can also download data and generate maps directly from the Census Bureau, sorted by a factor such as age of children in the household. Overlap these basic maps with a map of your best "champions" in each neighborhood. Those are the homes where you might want to hold an evening coffee about new programs that your school is offering or to try to attract new families to your school.

You can also purchase all kinds of data on interests and buying trends from data and marketing firms. For some school stakeholders, using consumer data will seem "icky" if not downright dirty. Why should schools have to play these games and advertise to families as if we were in the business of selling dish soap or soda? The fact is that many private schools have been doing this for years (or if not, they are starting to). Some public schools now have to also compete for customers, and using, at a minimum, free public data to help build a better picture of your current and potential customers is just good practice.

Activity III.7

Teachers Teaching Teachers (half-day–full day)

Purpose: Scaling change

Nothing is more powerful in helping schools shift their practice than creating opportunities for teachers to learn from practicing colleagues. A primary reason that school teams bring in "experts" or send their educators to far-away conferences is that they don't think they have the expertise that they need in-house. As your team gathers new ideas about their practice by getting connected on social media, webinars, and video chats, build a real culture of learning by routinely holding your own in-house Teachers Teaching Teachers events.

I recommend that at least once (and hopefully twice) a year, the entire faculty and administration participate in an on-site Teaching event. It should be at least a half-day long. It can be a combination of poster sessions and breakout workshops. A good rule of thumb is that breakouts should be between 50 and 90 minutes, and there should be enough offered such that attendance will average between 15 and 30 colleagues in each session.

Here is the key: Most teachers will initially say they can't or don't want to lead a breakout session. Overcome this by training and starting small. During some collaborative professional growth time, block out one hour for individuals or small teams of no more than three to do the following:

- Come up with an idea for a breakout session; this might be something they learned about at a conference or just something they are trying in their own classroom.

- If people struggle with finding an idea, start with this prompt: *Tell me about something you have done with your students that is probably different than what other teachers do; identify a time when your students were super-engaged and enthused about their learning. What were the keys to that? Tell me more!*

- Design a breakout session that is approximately 40 percent instructional and 60 percent active learning for the participants.

- Stand and give a 10-minute "sample" of the full breakout to another team or group of teams.

- Use the feedback to finalize your workshop plan.

With this short practice session, most educators realize that they *do* have something worthwhile to share and that leading or co-leading a one-hour active learning breakout for their colleagues is not hard—and is actually fun!

Want to really ramp this up? Have students design and lead breakout sessions for their teachers! And, after one to two years of holding in-house Teaching events, invite teachers and administrators from other schools or districts to join your Teaching event. You may charge a small fee or do it for free. Now your school is viewed as a leader in education innovation. Nothing will change the culture of a school faster than colleagues learning and gaining comfort from their peers and their students.

Activity III.8

Classroom Practicum (60 minutes)

Purpose: Scaling change through experiential learning

If, like many schools, your team creates a North Star that seeks a shift toward a more student-centric, student-owned learning process, then a chunk of your value-based transformation will involve actual implementation of a deeper learning pedagogy in the classroom. What does this actually look like? How is it different from what you are doing today? Teaching teams can easily help coach each other in how to build a deeper learning experience that will increasingly excite and engage their students.

- Carve out one hour of PD (professional development) time several times a year. Ask for volunteers (and then rotate through the entire faculty) to lead a 10- to 15-minute classroom activity that would change their own practice. Some themes to get started might include the following:

  ○ Engaging Students (you can find a list of suggestions on my Deeper Learning Cheat Sheet [2015] at my website, http://www.grantlichtman.com/resources/)

  ○ Use of Space (using the classroom and adjacent campus areas differently)

  ○ Individualized Learning (small-group and individually paced work)

- Break the faculty into teams of eight to 10. Each team goes to a different classroom. Mix up the teams so grade levels and subjects are *not* grouped together.

- In each classroom, three of the "volunteers" individually "teach" their 10- to 15-minute activity as if the other teachers were their students. After each one, the group gives feedback using the "I like, I wonder, what if" protocol. In this protocol, feedback is given *only* using one of these three phrases to start a sentence, and the receiver of feedback does not defend but only responds "thank you."

- Try to set a schedule such that every teacher presents a new learning experience and receives feedback at least once a year.

Activity III.9

Heat Mapping (30–60 minutes)

Purpose: Prioritizing and focusing innovation resources

When school groups create a North Star, the questions often become, "Where do we begin? What are the big things to tackle first? How can we avoid duplicating work, and how can we collaborate among different teams?" With multiple teams working on different areas of research or design challenges, it is helpful to create a graphical way to visualize areas where the work of these teams might overlap. I developed this "Heat Mapping" protocol (see Figure F) with Kate Saunders at the Tilton School when we were trying to gather common areas of focus among nine different design teams working on areas as disparate as student assessment, faculty professional growth and evaluation, and boarding school life.

- First, draw a *big* wall-sized circle. In the middle of it, state a "big challenge," such as "enrollment" or "a deeper learning experience" or "hiring and retaining the best faculty."

- Around the edges of the big circle, post big ideas from each of the research or design teams: lessons learned, limiting conditions, or key challenges that will inform the "big challenge" in the center.

- Then, the individual research/design teams hang elements of their research or prototypes near the guiding elements on the perimeter of the circle. There are no right answers to this, and some teams will want to post a single design element on two or more perimeter locations; this is fine.

- The result is a visual grouping of ideas around elements of the problem you are trying to solve. As the teams start to work, they can easily see where multiple teams have generated overlapping interests, and they know to coordinate in these areas as prototypes of new projects take shape.

Figure F Heat Map of Places to Focus Next Steps

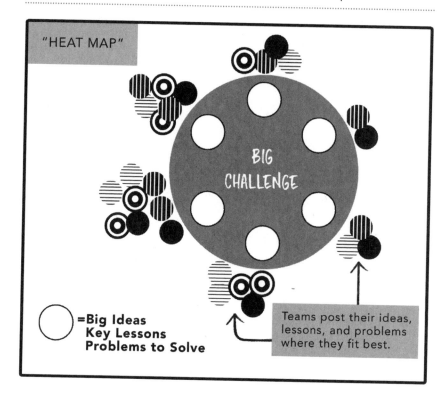

Activities Useful in Any Setting

The activities in this first group don't necessarily accompany any one chapter or section in the book. They apply to multiple opportunities as your team practices develop.

Activity IV.1

Effective Teams (20–40 minutes)

Purpose: Building team capacity and effectiveness

The great news is that effective teams can tremendously boost value-rich innovation in schools. More great news is that most educators have participated in high-performing teams at some point in their lives, usually on a ball field when they were kids. The bad news is that most educators have *not* been trained to form and participate in effective teams during their career or at their school. There are library and bookstore shelves and an entire consulting industry dedicated to creating and managing effective teams. Schools can work with and study all of these materials . . . or give groups of faculty, administrators, and/or students about 20 minutes together.

Have groups separate a piece of flip chart paper or a section of whiteboard into two columns and brainstorm for 10 to 15 minutes about these topics:

- Characteristics of ineffective teams
- Characteristics of effective teams

We have found that, in most cases, school groups will collectively nail about 90 percent of what you will find in the books and workshops dedicated to this topic. The fact is that most of us have experience working on teams across the effectiveness spectrum, and there is little disagreement when people share these experiences.

Once groups have identified what it takes to act as an effective team, then the real work starts: committing to a set of norms and actually sticking to them. This is where training is invaluable, as most educators have not had skills training in creating and sustaining effective teams. Start with a Google search of Tuckman's Stages of Group Development, and consider bringing in professionals to help coach during the early years of team-based work.

Activity IV.2

Stop Sitting (0 minutes)

Purpose: Increase energy and engagement of any group

Meeting time at schools is overwhelmingly static time. Around conference tables, in offices, at faculty meetings, and even in interactive workshops, most of us are sitting most of the time—much like the students in our classrooms. In any kind of group-based activity, find opportunities to get up, move around, work on the floor or on a wall, or leave the workshop space for a 20-minute activity—go outside and use dry erase markers on windows! Sitting down, particularly in a long block of time, is the *least* conducive method to achieving good collaboration and maintaining creative energy. Most of us have been trained in very static learning environments; we wait for permission to leave our seats. Get up!

Activity IV.3

Why We Meet? (less than 1 minute)

Purpose: Increase group efficiency

At the start of any meeting, ask your colleagues, "Why are we meeting?" At a minimum, the person who called the meeting should know and be able to explain in a sentence. Hopefully, others know as well. If there is any hesitation, perhaps that means that the meeting was less than necessary.

A great opportunity to ask and answer this question is at the start of a faculty meeting. If faculty meet in order to give the principal or division head an opportunity to get up and talk or to pass along information that could have been sent in an e-mail or posted in the Learning Management System, you should be redirecting some of those time blocks to the kind of interactive activities that can only take place in face-to-face meetings (you know, the kind that most school teams say they don't have enough time for!).

Activity IV.4

Ban the Negativity! (less than 1 minute)

Purpose: Shifting group mindset

The phrase *Yes, but* . . . is particularly hurtful to team-based innovation. Think about how many times someone starts a sentence with those two words and then proceeds to find a reason why something *can't* be done. (Seriously— keep track of this for a day or a week of meetings and the frequency will frighten you. Breaking teammates of this habit can be like getting a sailor to stop swearing!) I know several school leaders who have banned this phrase's use. Each time you get someone to rephrase the thought using *Yes, and* . . . is an opportunity to *build on* the thinking and work of others rather than finding reasons to reject it.

Similarly, challenge teams to avoid the terms *us* and *them* when referring to people who operate in different school silos. This is particularly relevant in conversations with teaching faculty and administrators when one group is referring to the other. Using *us* and *them* is a convenient way to place blame on "the other" rather than seeing the group of school stakeholders as a community with common purpose.

Activity IV.5

Keep/Stop/Start (15 minutes)

Purpose: Addition by subtraction

I have seen versions of this activity pop up increasingly among change leaders. This simple exercise allows teams to quickly identify opportunities to free up resources that they have previously thought were untouchable. I generally use this protocol during the Activities stage of a prototyping or Logic Model exercise when teams are in that sticky phase of trying to design just *how* they are going to implement a significant change. It is a simple, powerful tool to help people realize that strategy and good design are as much about what you choose *not* to do as what you choose *to* do.

Section pieces of flip chart paper or the whiteboard into three columns, labeled *Keep*, *Stop*, and *Start*. Using either sticky notes or just writing in the columns, teams brainstorm items for each column relative to the project they are imagining:

- What is absolutely required that we keep from the past in order to make this pilot successful?

- What can we stop doing to free up resources that we need for this new program or project?

- What would we start for the first time if this pilot were adopted?

Where there is not consensus, it is good to have a "parking lot," so the team does not get bogged down arguing about a small handful of issues that may have to be decided later. Again, I like using sticky notes because it gives the team the opportunity to question the placement of notes in each column and potentially move or remove a note after discussion.

Activity IV.6

Gallery Walks or Finding "Lego Pieces" (10 minutes)

Purpose: Gathering ideas to stimulate creative prototyping

Just as we can build an infinite array of strange objects by finding new ways to combine a relatively few types of Lego blocks, value-rich innovation often is found in combining old pieces in new ways.

The Gallery Walk is a critical tool. Once a group has papered the walls, whiteboards, and windows with sticky notes, flip chart paper, and sketches, take a few minutes for the group to walk around and take notes of major themes or specific ideas that resonate with them. The goal of Gallery Walk is *not* that each person sees and studies every item that is on the walls. The idea is that groups will wander about, see what other groups have been thinking, and then come back to their own working team with some new insights or major takeaways to share. Everyone brings those ideas back to their table, jots them down on sticky notes, and shares them; they should literally the put them in a pile in the middle of the table. These are the "Lego pieces" the team should use in the next step of a design challenge, ultimately prototyping something new for the school.

Activity IV.7

Two Exit Tickets: 3-2-1 and WW/DD (3 minutes)

Purpose: Gather rapid feedback and focus on user needs

A big part of change is developing a culture of honest feedback. Educators tend to be congenial, which means they often don't tell you what you need to hear. We need honest feedback about whatever activity just took place so we can improve on the experience the next time. Try one of these two protocols:

- 3-2-1 is a common feedback protocol. Before leaving the room, attendees jot down on cards or sticky notes *three* takeaways that they hope will stick with them; *two* things that resonate or "square" with their own views; and *one* thing that they are still wondering or worrying about.

- WW/DD is something I learned from Julie Wilson. Before leaving, attendees post at least one note on a "What Worked for You Today" list and at least one note on the "Do Differently Next Time" board. The next time the group meets—be that the next day or month—a great place to start is a summary of what you, as the convener, heard from this feedback.

Appendix II

Schools, Networks, Conferences, and Book Suggestions to Help Discover "The Possible"

In Appendix II, I want to share three additional sets of resources:

- Schools

- Networks and gatherings

- Books you may not have read

Schools That "Do School" Differently

In my books and on my website, I am always torn about whether or not to share lists of "exemplar" schools or programs. Doing so is full of pitfalls: No one person (and certainly not I) has seen or heard of many of the great school and program exemplars that exist today, or will by the time you read this. Five or ten years ago, this would have been a short list; now it is very long, growing longer every month, and I can't pretend to keep up. So there will be school teams that are rightfully upset at not being included; I apologize!

A second pitfall is that I have not visited or vetted many of these schools myself. By posting a name here, I am not vouching for them, nor am I suggesting that their version of "school" is a fit for your community. They are in my archive of schools to keep an eye on because they were mentioned in a blog post or by a colleague, and I probably have visited their website before including them on my own archive list.

A third pitfall is that some of these exemplars may not be any longer! Not all pilots are successful over time. Some schools may have launched along a trajectory of truly differentiated value and flamed out or taken a time-out or a different path.

Finally, while it is tempting to try to put these schools in "categories" of innovation, many would fit into more than one, and they are changing all the time.

With those pitfalls in mind, I still am frequently asked by school leaders where they can look to find those people and schools that have been down a path of transformation. The strength of our current tipping point is that we have so many schools that are making some of these changes that we can learn from each other and *not* all reinvent the wheel. The power of this upside seems to outweigh the pitfalls, so here are some schools that I have archived over the last several years. Reach out, research, and learn as you will!

- Design 39 Campus, Poway, CA

- Harrisburg School District, Sioux Falls, SD

- Kettle Moraine Unified School District, WI

- Lindsay School District, CA
    - Del Lago Academy, Escondido, CA
    - Elizabeth Forward School District, PA
    - Holy Family Academy, Pittsburgh, PA
    - Albermarle Tech: The Center for Creativity and Innovation, Charlottesville, VA
    - Vista Innovation and Design Academy (VIDA), Vista, CA
    - High Tech High, Middle, and Elementary Schools, CA
    - Science Leadership Academy, Pittsburgh, PA
    - Mount Vernon Presbyterian, Atlanta, GA
    - Parish Episcopal School, Dallas, TX
    - Khan Lab School, Mt. View, CA
    - Delphian Schools, Sheridan, OR
    - IowaBIG, Cedar Falls, IA
    - Winston Thurston School, Pittsburgh, PA
    - Kingsway College School, Toronto, ON
    - The Downtown School, Seattle, WA
    - Hobsonville Point Secondary School, Auckland, NZ
    - Synapse School, Menlo Park, CA
    - Paulo Freire Freedom Schools Tuscon, AZ
    - Workspace Education, Bethel, CT
    - THINK Global School, New York, NY
    - Intrinsic Schools, Chicago, IL
    - UT OnRamps, Austin, TX
    - Quest to Learn, New York, NY
    - Wildwood IB Magnet, Chicago, IL
    - Maine Township HS District, Park Ridge, IL
    - Bennett Day School, Chicago, IL
    - Birmingham Covington, Bloomfield Hills, MI
    - Inquiry Hub Secondary, Coquitlam, BC
    - E3 Civic High, San Diego, CA
    - Acton Academy, Austin, TX
    - Northern Cass School District, Hunter, ND
    - The Academy Group, Chicago, IL

- Cristo Rey Network, www.cristoreynetwork.org
- Summit Schools
- Blyth-Templeton Academy, Washington, DC
- Achievement School District, Memphis, TN
- Brooklyn Lab School, Brooklyn, NY
- Success Academy Charter Schools, New York, NY
- Matchbook Learning, www.matchbooklearning.com
- USC Hybrid High, Los Angeles, CA
- San Francisco University High School, San Francisco, CA
- Bridge International Academies, www.bridgeinternationalacademies.com
- AltSchool, www.altschool.com
- Lincoln School, Providence, RI
- University Prep, Seattle, WA
- Bay School, San Francisco, CA
- Ashoka Changemaker Schools, www.ashoka.org
- BASIS Independent (Charter) Schools, www.basised.com
- Riverpoint Academy, Spokane, WA
- Teton Science School, Jackson Hole, WY
- Sun Valley Community School, Sun Valley, ID
- D-Tech High School, Redwood City, CA
- NuVu Studio, Cambridge, MA
- The STEAM Center at Brooklyn Navy Yard, Brooklyn, NY
- Epic High, Queens, NY
- CART, Fresno, CA
- Cornerstone Academy for Social Action, Bronx, NY
- Nueva School, Hillsborough/San Mateo, CA
- Catlin Gabel, Portland, OR
- Putney School, Putney, VT
- Independent School of Winchester, VA
- The Apollo School (part of Central York High School), PA
- Michigan Public Museum School, MI
- Midland School, Los Olivos, CA
- St. John's School, Houston, TX

- The Stone Independent School, Lancaster, PA

- Whittle Studio and School, Washington, DC

- Avenues: The World School, New York City, NY

- Powderhouse Studios, Somerville, MA

- Millennium School, San Francisco, CA

- Lab Atlanta, Atlanta, GA

- Mead School District, Spokane, WA

- Cajon Valley Union School District, El Cajon, CA

- Hawken School, Cleveland, OH

- Brightworks, San Francisco, CA

- GEMS Education Schools, www.gemseducation.com

- KɔSchool, Austin, TX

- Mysa School, Bethesda, MD

- Wildwood School, Los Angeles, CA

- MC2 Charters, NH, www.mc2school.org

- Blue Hill Harbor School, Blue Hill, ME

- Leominster Center for Excellence, Leominster, MA

- Via Getting Smart, www.gettingsmart.com

  - 15 school districts worth visiting

  - 100 middle and high schools worth visiting

  - 70 elementary and middle schools worth visiting

Networks, Gatherings, and Other Leads

Formal networks of schools, and both physical and virtual gathering points, often have more resources and are often more sustainable than individual schools. There are knowledge networks like Edutopia, and there are networks of practice like Deeper Learning, EdCamps, or XQ America. You may want to search these networks before focusing on specific schools. Find those that overlap with your North Star, and find some member schools nearby to start your research and connectivity.

I also include here some of the longer-running meet-ups and conferences that seem to consistently provide active learning experiences about how you can "do school" differently. Many of the networks have annual conferences for members as well as some for nonmembers. I am not advocating or advertising for any of these, and of course, they might well vary from year to year and over time in terms of their focus and performance.

Networks and Consortia

- Education ReImagined
- EdVisions
- Envision Education
- Liberated Learners
- Big Picture Learning Network
- Transcend Education
- Innovative Schools
- Students at The Center.org
- EdLeader21
- Independent Curriculum Group
- XQ America
- Hackable High Schools
- Remake Learning
- EdCamps Foundation
- New Tech Network
- Coalition of Essential Schools
- Canadian Association of Independent Schools
- Design Learning Network
- Cohort 21
- CompetencyWorks.org
- CWRA
- Assessment for Learning Project
- Performance Assessment of Competency Education
- Mastery Transcript Consortium
- EduCause
- Transform Education
- California Performance Assessment Collaborative
- New York Performance Standards Consortium
- Innovation Lab Network
- New England Secondary School Consortium
- Performance Assessment Bank
- PARCC
- Smarter Balanced Assessment Consortium

- Next Generation Learning Challenges
- Institute for Personalized Learning, CESA #1, Wisconsin
- Educators for Social Responsibility

Conferences, Gatherings, and Innovation Centers

- 39X (Design 39 Campus)
- CTTL (Education Neuroscience, St. Andrew's School)
- Traverse Conferences
- FUSE Conference (Mt. Vernon Presbyterian)
- CAIS Strategic Change Accelerator
- EdCamps Foundation
- Schools of Opportunity (National Education Policy Center)
- EduCon (Science Leadership Academy)
- Harvard Project Zero
- Hawken Entrepreneurs
- Noble Impact
- Woodrow Wilson Academy of Teaching and Learning
- Center for Transformational Leadership (Dallas)
- iNacol
- Deeper Learning (High Tech High)
- Harvard Transforming Learning Deeper Learning Program
- iNoted
- New Hampshire PACE
- Nueva School Conferences
- Forum for Education and Democracy
- Center for Education Renewal

Resources Related to College Admissions and Education Schools

- Turning the Tide
- Mastery Transcript Consortium
- Coalition for College Access, Affordability, and Success
- Deans for Impact (deansforimpact.org)
- Competency-Based Education Network

Resources Related to Curriculum and Instruction

- Edutopia
- Khan Academy
- CK–12 Foundation
- The Teaching Channel
- RedesignU.org
- Mindshift KQED
- Hewlett Foundation Open Education Resources
- Sanford Institute, University of Arizona (online teacher training)
- TES Connect (UK)
- N4L (NZ)
- Classworks
- Center for Curriculum Redesign

Resources Related to Design, MakerSpaces, and Learning Environments

- Punahou School Learning Commons
- MVIFI HIVE Playbook
- Nueva School, CA
- Makerspace Playbook
- Beaver Country Day, Boston, MA
- MakerEd.org
- Hillbrook School iLab

Online Learning

- Stanford Online High School
- K12.com
- Online School for Girls
- Connections Academy
- Global Online Academy
- Online Learning Consortium
- Coursera
- edX
- iNACOL
- Udacity

Design Thinking

- Stanford d.school

- Mt. Vernon Institute for Innovation, GA

- Design 39 Campus, Poway Unified, CA

- Design Thinking Resources Guide

- AK12DC (GA)

- Tools at Schools

Books You May Not Have Read

What follows are some books (and what I believe are their authors' key messages) that you may not have read and might want to add to your reading list. Some I have cited in this book, and all have informed my understanding of how the world is changing, how organizations effectively deal with change, and how schools in particular are finding success in this evolutionary environment. These are not all of the books on my "must read" list; I have listed those here that I think may have escaped your radar screen.

Simple Rules (2015) Donald Sull and Kathleen Eisenhardt

Simple is almost always better than complicated. Organizations like schools can create a set of simple rules or guidelines to decide complex questions, and the efficiencies are enormous.

Key Takeaways

- The authors cite many examples of simple rules; here are two to give you an idea of what simple rules are:

  - Prior to WWII, battlefield injuries were treated at field hospitals largely on a first-come, first served basis. Fatality rates were staggering. Doctors came up with the *triage* system of sorting patients into four groups based on simple guidelines that could be very quickly measured upon patient arrival, focusing scarce resources where they could do the most good for the most patients. Survivability rates of battlefield injuries among those who make it to a field hospital using triage rules have risen ever since.

  - Athletic trainers for Stanford football found that just three eating habit guidelines were more beneficial to the entire team than the set of complex workout and diet rules they replaced: Eat a good breakfast, hydrate, and eat as much as you want of things you can pick, grow, or kill.

- Simple rules help us to decide some of the boundary conditions before we start solving a problem. Here is a concrete example that many schools are struggling with: We want to find time in the daily schedule for . . . (take your pick: mindfulness, balance, reflection, global programs, capstones, new courses, more sleep for students, teacher collaboration, etc.). But there are a limited number of minutes in the day. And everyone has his or her own pet need or bit of turf to protect. How do we decide what to add, what to keep, and what to let go?

- Some simple rules might sound like this:

  - "The social and emotional needs of students will take precedence over higher performance on tests."

  - "Time will be apportioned based on student identification and pursuit of knowledge, not predetermined subject areas."

  - "Learning takes place where knowledge resides, not necessarily within a classroom."

Schools and the students they serve are not all the same, so the rules will be different. By creating sets of guiding rules like these, though, we will make decisions, some of which are uncomfortable, based on what we think is most important overall, not what is most expedient in the moment.

iGen (2017) Jean Twenge

Research-based insights into how today's superconnected generation is very different from previous boomers, Gen-Xers, and millennials.

Key Takeaways

- **iGeners are not in a rush to grow up**. They are more likely to want to stay at home (partly because they cannot afford to both pay off college debt and buy or rent a house on low-paying jobs) and less likely to do some of the "grown-up" things that past generations have rushed into: dating, marrying, drinking, drugs, and taking both good and bad risks.

- **They are growing up online and are intimately attached to their phones in time and space.** This tether is significantly impacting how young people feel about themselves: body image, social groups, feedback online, and so on. Teens hang out with real people less and spend much more of their day looking at, and interacting with, a small screen.

- **They read less and do not follow current events.** Despite their attachment to the Internet, they don't keep up with current events and are shockingly ignorant of the physical, economic, and political world around them.

- **They are "mentally fragile" and more likely to be depressed, with higher rates of a wide variety of mental health issues.** Much of this can be tied to screen time and lack of human contact. They are also the generation that has been subjected to overprotective helicopter parents, which amplifies the anxiety put onto kids by parents who constantly worry about their safety and future.

- **They are more concerned with safety, which is a good thing when it comes to lower incidents of risky behavior.** But this also seems to be the reason that so many students are uncomfortable with people and settings that run counter to their own worldview (college students who, for example, do not believe free speech necessarily extends to those who they believe are saying things that threaten their own views). They believe that we all have the right to be sheltered from ideas and people who disagree with us since their home lives tended to shelter them more from these real-world crosscurrents.

- It was fewer than 20 years ago (which passes quickly in school time) that we were spending huge amounts of focus and money on getting our students more connected with evolving technologies. Now it appears that we should be discussing "unplugged" hours and days at school so that our students learn how to be human in ways that are not controlled by addictive "iDevices."

Creativity, Inc. (2014) Edwin Catmull

Creativity, Inc., by Pixar cofounder Edwin Catmull, is an absolute must read for anyone starting or running a company, any manager, and pretty much everyone in education. It is the story of how Pixar was born, how it came to be one of the most successful companies on the planet, why it is an organization where really smart, talented people desperately want to work, and how it continues to evolve to pursue, and actually achieve, that one key goal of making a great product.

Key Takeaways

- How creative organizations leverage people:
  - Constantly push people to contribute.
  - Hire people who have potential to grow.
  - If people feel they are not free to suggest things, you lose.
  - Nothing shuts down alternative viewpoints as much as being convinced you are right.
  - Finding and fixing problems is everyone's job.
- How creative organizations leverage process:
  - Everybody should be able to talk to anybody.
  - Protect the future, not the past.

- Process is not a goal. The goal is a great product.
- Don't accidentally make stability a goal. Balance is more important than stability.
- Crises are not lamentable; they test and demonstrate an organization's values.
- How creative organizations leverage risk and failure:
  - The first conclusions we draw from failure are usually wrong.
  - The cost of preventing failures is almost always greater than the cost of fixing them.
  - Failure is a necessary consequence of doing something new.
  - The desire for everything to run smoothly is a false goal.

Most schools don't place a high value on creating; they see their mission in terms of passing along existing knowledge, which is, to be sure, a *big* part of our mission. But creativity is the lifeblood of value-rich innovation. Customers are going to choose a school where "creativity" and "greatness" are the norm.

This Is Marketing (2018) Seth Godin

Effective marketing in our modern world demands we understand our customers' worldview and desires so we can connect with them.

Key Takeaways

- "The heart and soul of a thriving enterprise is the irrational pursuit of becoming irresistible."
- "People don't want what you make. They want what it will do for them. They want the way it will make them feel."
- "Modern society, urban society, the society of the Internet, the arts, and innovation are all built primarily on affiliation, not dominion. This type of status is not 'I'm better.' It's 'I'm connected. I'm family.' And in an economy based on connection, not manufacturing, being a trusted member of the family is priceless."
- "If we merely try to fill a hole in the market, we're doomed to a cycle of rearview-mirror behavior. We're nothing but a commodity in the making, always wary of our competition. We have no choice but to be driven by scarcity, focused on maintaining or perhaps slightly increasing our market share. The alternative is to find and build and earn your story, the arc of the change you seek to produce. This is a generative posture, one based on possibility, not scarcity."
- "When you're marketing change, you're offering a new emotional state, a step closer to the dreams and desires of your customers, not a widget."

Social Physics (2014) Alex Pentland

Good ideas spread and both individual and group performance are enhanced when we build social networking pathways into our collaborative interactions.

Key Takeaways

- **Ideas and creative flow are enhanced** when social learning within a peer group leads to development of norms and social pressures to enforce those norms.

- **The most productive individuals in a group do the following:**
  - Build and maintain stronger engagement with the people in their network
  - Increase diversity within their networks
  - Spend more time looking at what others are doing

- **"The best strategy for learning** is to spend 90% of our efforts on exploration; that is, finding and copying others who appear to be doing well. The remaining 10% should be spent on individual experimentation and thinking things through."

- **Social network incentives** are almost four times more effective at increasing individual and group performance than traditional incentives, and performance is maintained at higher levels even after the incentives disappear.

- **The largest factor in predicating group intelligence** is the equality of conversational turn taking. Individual intelligence, personality, and skill matter less to group performance than the pattern of idea flow.

Building School 2.0 (2015)
Chris Lehmann and Zac Chase

This is a profound and insightful guidebook on how to create the schools we need from the founders of Science Leadership Academy, one of the iconic public high schools in America.

Key Takeaways

- Overtly borrowing the template of Martin Luther, there are 95 theses in the book, each comprising a few pages of honest, pithy, and, in my opinion, absolutely spot-on arguments for why each thesis is a pathway to great learning for more kids with diverse life experiences.

- Each short chapter winds up with several equally direct, succinct, practical activities or actions that educators can implement the very next day to begin to shift their own practice and/or that of those around them.

- A few examples:
  - "Vision must live in practice."
  - "'What's good' is better than 'what's new.'"
  - "Humility matters."
  - "Don't admire the problem."
  - "Stop deficit model thinking."
  - "There are no sick or snow days."
- Each thesis is weighty, yet the authors engagingly convey key elements of *what*, *why*, and *what to do about it* in very few words.
- They call on the reader to open to a page each day or week, reflect on the narrative and advice, and then just try some things that are proven to work.

Neuroteach (2016) Glenn Whitman and Ian Kelleher

Whitman and Kelleher tell us how the exploding field of brain science is impacting what we know, how we learn, and how K–12 educators can take advantage of a future that is evolving for us in real time.

Key Takeaways

- Written by everyday classroom teachers who have been deeply involved with research into cognitive neuroscience at leading universities.
- Elevates each reader's current Mind, Brain, and Education science mindset, knowledge, and research to practice translation skills.
- Bridges the gap between active research into cognitive neuroscience and what takes place in classrooms every day.
- Provides "next day" MBE science research informed strategies that can be applied to the design of schools, curriculum, and work with each individual student (regardless of school type or geographic location).
- Models a Science of Learning to help prepare adult learner-teachers, focusing on attention, memory, metacognition, feedback, assessment, engagement, dual coding, cognitive load, homework, and the connection between emotion and cognition.
- Provides links for teachers to practice with a virtual microlearning experience, Neuroteach Global.

Team of Teams (2015) Stanley McChrystal

Fast-paced dynamic challenges require that we structure leadership and organizations to become vastly more fluid and responsive.

Key Takeaways

- "Adaptability, not efficiency, must become our central competency."

- "In complex environments, resilience often spells success, while even the most brilliantly engineered solutions are often insufficient or counterproductive."

- Effective "teams of teams" exhibit three main characteristics:

  - Strong lateral connections—Every individual does not have a relationship with every other individual. But everyone knows someone on every team.

  - Systemic understanding—Every team possesses a holistic understanding of the interaction between the moving parts.

  - Decentralized control—Leaders provide information so that subordinates armed with context, understanding, and connectivity can take the initiative and make decisions.

The Human Side of Changing Education (2018)
Julie Wilson

Many school leaders know that problem solving, collaboration, and creativity are integral parts of a school's DNA, but they don't know how to build these strengths.

Key Takeaways

- When we ask schools to change, we are asking human beings to change. This requires special tools and a human-centered approach.

- Leaders can learn to make sense of their challenging change journeys and accelerate effective implementation.

- With this practical framework that includes human-centered tools, resources, and mini case studies, readers learn to navigate and succeed on their unique path of change.

- Resistance to change is to be expected, and we know how to get through it.

- There are at least three different kinds of change strategies, and effective school leaders know when to use which one.

- All individuals and new teams go through the "messy middle" of change, where real transformation happens; skilled teams come out of this stronger and more effective.

- We can change the heart of the school system by enabling the hearts and minds of those who make schools work.

The Inevitable (2016) Kevin Kelly

From someone who has had a front-row seat to the birth and growth of the information age, this book offers a clear vision of the future that is already here.

Key Takeaways

- Kelly cofounded *Wired* magazine in 1993 and has had a front-row seat to the birth and explosion of the Information Age. In *The Inevitable*, he focuses on the *forces* of change, not the products and services that continue to flow into our lives.

- These forces, all empowered as verbs, include becoming, cognifying, flowing, accessing, sharing, filtering, and more. They are the evolutionary factors that will increasingly determine outcomes of many of our most human goals and ambitions: success, happiness, fulfillment, and satisfaction.

- We are already experiencing the rapid evolution of a global social neural network, (the cognitosphere or metaverse) that empowers and rewards the creation and free flow of knowledge vastly more than the transaction of knowledge as a commodity.

- While the development of technologies—screens, networks, filters, artificial intelligence, storage, and more—absorbs our daily lives, these ever-more-rapid iterations are now a given and put the inevitable development of hardware and software into the back seat. The front seat belongs to how *our lives change* as technologies increasingly become just another part of the ecosystem.

- Much of what sounds like science fiction in the book is not; it is already here, or at least on the immediate horizon.

- The rate of change in technology is always increasing as various technologies combine. It is reasonable to assume that AI (artificial intelligence) will be part of our everyday lives within the next decade.

Design Thinking for School Leaders (2018) Alyssa Gallagher and Kami Thordarson

This text provides concrete steps for school leaders to use the tools of design thinking when leading their teams through changes that can be both exciting and also uncomfortable.

Key Takeaways

- It provides both theory and clear, highly practical guidelines for how school leaders can shift from being mere managers to becoming design-inspired leaders.

- Design thinking is firmly rooted in understanding the needs of the user. This book grounds the work of transforming schools in the key design element of empathy for school users (students, teachers, parents, and the broader community).

- There are at least five specific design-based roles to help leaders identify opportunities for positively impacting students, teachers, districts, parents, and the community:
  - Opportunity Seeker, who helps teams overcome inertia and fear of the unknown by shifting conversations from problem solving to problem finding.
  - Experience Architect, who specializes in understanding the changing needs of learners; both designs and curates learning experiences that rise to meet those needs.
  - Rule Breaker, who confidently challenges the way things are "always" done; finds and supports change agents in the school; models risk-taking so others will follow with optimism that change is empowered, even in the face of failure.
  - Producer, who is not frustrated by the status quo and school bureaucracy; gets things done and creates rapid learning cycles for teams.
  - Storyteller, who is the critical communicator who captures the hearts and minds of a community and helps others to act as effective ambassadors of change.

Timeless Learning (2018) Ira Socol, Pam Moran, and Chad Ratliff

In this, you will find a primer in how to change schools, written by visionary, veteran education leaders of one of the most challenging, innovative, and diverse districts in America.

Key Takeaways

- No actions are more important than developing and reinforcing children's sense of agency, the value of their voices, and their potential to influence their own communities. We simply must include students more in decisions we make about our schools and in the decisions that they can and should make about their own learning experience.
- When we are able to see clearly what is happening with children in and outside of schools, we are able to learn how to take rapid yet deeply considered actions to change the educational system we have inherited.
- To increase the likelihood of success for all learners, educators' decisions must reflect values that support equity, accessibility, inclusivity, empathy, cultural responsiveness, and connected relationships.

- A school community's culture will determine to a great extent whether its inhabitants thrive or fail. The culture, in turn, represents the ecology of each school. That ecology is crafted not just by every space, not just by every in-class and homework assignment, not just by the schedule, not just by the grading system, but also through every word spoken or shown to every student, by every teacher's tone of voice or facial expression.

Our Kids (2015) Robert Putnam

Americans have always believed that those who have talent and try hard will succeed, but this central tenet of the American Dream seems no longer true.

Key Takeaways

- Young people growing up in America in the 1950s and 1960s were often able to live lives better than those of their parents. This is no longer the case for large segments of the American population.

- America is becoming more rigid and less mobile between economic classes: in neighborhoods, schools, and jobs. Upper classes live relatively charmed, isolated lives with many opportunities that are extremely remote for those in lower economic classes.

- Children growing up in both rich and poor neighborhoods used to be viewed by adults as "ours," looking out for the well-being of kids who were not their own and often did not look like their own. Neighborhoods have become increasingly isolated, and students from less-advantaged neighborhoods are increasingly less likely to find a pathway out of poverty.

The primary difference in opportunity between those of this generation who succeed in education and job opportunities is the family/social safety net. Children who lack this safety net are much less likely to survive or thrive beyond one major setback like an illness, death of parents, doing poorly in school, or a minor brush with the law.

Creative Confidence (2013) Tom Kelley and David Kelley

The power and processes of design thinking are outlined by two of the founders and most profound influencers in how we find and solve problems.

Key Takeaways

- Tom and David Kelley are founders of global design thinking leader IDEO. David was a key driver behind the rise of the Stanford d.school, which in turn has influenced nearly every major college and university around the world to develop schools that merge science, engineering, and design.

- Design thinking is a process whereby solution makers look for the best solution to the biggest problem. They empathetically engage users in order to ensure that creative solutions meet the needs of the users, not just the designers.

- Design thinking is an idea/thinking/creative/synthesis accelerator. Teachers and students who are handed these simple tools explode into ownership of their own learning. School community stakeholders who are allowed to design solutions become vastly more invested in implementing their designs.

- Within the context of education, design thinking is a modern interpretation or reawakening of what John Dewey and the other giants of the Progressive Era taught us more than a century ago: We all learn and gain confidence by experience, empathy, engagement, pursuit of passion, collaboration, action, trial, and failure.

The Nature of the Future (2013) Marina Gorbis

We are experiencing rapid development of lower-cost, more-personalized alternatives to products and services, including education.

Key Takeaways

- The evolution of systems that facilitate the flow of knowledge and information is occurring across nearly every sector of commerce and human interaction.

- Wildly disruptive innovations like iTunes, Uber, Airbnb, online shopping, and open-source coding are all examples of the development of products and services that bypass traditional sources by creating personalized connections that do not require a middleman to engage in commerce or social interactions.

- We see the introduction of such flow facilitators in education as technology speeds up the creation, access, and management of knowledge.

- We now find many examples of companies, technologies, organizations, and individuals who are already successfully bypassing traditional school frameworks to deliver knowledge and the learning experience more efficiently, faster, and customized to the individual.

- What Gorbis calls a "socialstructed" world rewards the combination of initiative, passion, social connections, and the drive to build new things outside of existing institutions, ultimately with more flexible and resilient results.

Jobs to Be Done (2016) Anthony Ulwick

This text provides a widely used model for understanding why customers choose the products and services they do and is a new tool for schools that are in increasingly competitive marketplaces.

Key Takeaways

- "Most people would say they buy a lawnmower 'to cut the grass,' and this is true. But if a lawnmower company examines a higher purpose of cutting the grass, say to 'keep the grass low and beautiful at all times,' then it might forgo some efforts to make better lawnmowers in lieu of developing a genetically engineered grass seed that never needs to be cut."

- The jobs that schools and other organizations are hired to do fall into two categories:

  - Functional job aspects—These are the practical requirements that customers have that drive them to purchase goods and services.

  - Emotional job aspects—These are more "subjective customer requirements related to feelings and perception."

- A point that is highly relevant to schools today: "If your industry is mainly focused on the functional aspect of the job to be done, then differentiate yourself with the emotional aspect."

- The goal of innovation is to grow the value of the organization. JTBD (jobs to be done) practice creates a system by which we can better judge which innovations will actually result in more positive value as seen by the customers.

The Death of Expertise (2017) Tom Nichols

The rise of social media, political polarization, and differentiated media audiences has created the condition where fact-based learning is at serious risk.

Key Takeaways

- A key element of learning for centuries has been the reliance on experts who have invested enormous time, money, and intellectual resources in gaining knowledge and understanding that is deeper, more detailed, and often more nuanced than that of nonexperts.

- Because we disagree about how those facts might be used, the antiexpert factions claim they do not exist. We have reached the point at which everyone becomes an expert on everything.

- Highly vocal and politically potent groups of Americans from a range of the political spectrum increasingly decry almost any evidence-based argument coming from "elitist" experts when such expertise is contrary to their political or social viewpoint.

- Experts are not infallible, but they are vastly more accurate at describing the realities of the world around us than are lay people.

- Real experts are smart enough to know they are not always right and diligent enough to know how to get closer to "right" the next time. Those who decry the value of expertise because they don't agree with or want to hear the conclusions, are not.

- The rise of social media has created the condition in which all people, regardless of actual expertise, can access and influence large numbers of people without demonstrating actual knowledge of subject or facts to back up the arguments that they make. Many lay people give as much or more credence to nonexpert entertainment, sports, and other popular figures than they do to actual experts.

The Space (2018) Hare and Dillon

You will find ideas, concepts, and resources for educators to reimagine schools and classrooms and to design modern learning spaces that support excellent learning.

Key Takeaways

- Intentional classroom design enhances both engagement and joy in learning. If there is a key to transforming our schools, it is to refocus on student engagement in the learning process, and simple space design and usage can have real impact.

- Thoughtful space reconfiguration is done with the students and not for the students. Having students engage in how their learning space is used is, in itself, an exercise in active, relevant learning.

- Learning space design accelerates excellent instructional design. We don't change physical spaces without rebuilding the instructional practices that will take place in the new space. Pedagogy must always be at the heart of what we do in schools; new spatial configurations make these changes possible, but only if we are intentional about it.

- Classrooms have been set up for too long based on inertia and tradition. Most classroom configurations have not changed in years or decades and are, in fact, modeled after what classrooms looked and acted like when the teachers were students themselves. The simple act of questioning the physical configurations of classrooms prompts teachers to dig into their pedagogical goals.

- Small changes have real impact on student focus and achievement. Simple, inexpensive changes to things like furniture style and placement and what is on the walls can have demonstrable positive results.

References

Almquist, E., Senior, J., & Bloch, N. (2016). Elements of value. *Harvard Business Review*. Retrieved from https://hbr.org/2016/09/the-elements-of-value

Baghai, M., Coley, S., & White, D. (1999). *The alchemy of growth*. New York, NY: McKinsey and Company.

Business Performance Innovation Network Study. (2015). Retrieved from http://www .bpinetwork.org/thought-leadership/studies

Catmull, E. (2014). *Creativity, inc.* New York, NY: Random House.

Chandraker, A., Houmes, H., Hogg, J., & Reilly, C. (2018). *Innovation as unusual*. Retrieved from https://www.paconsulting.com/globalassets/downloads/pa-innovation-report-2016.pdf

Christensen, C., Anthony, S., Berstell, G., & Nitterhouse, D. (2007). Finding the right job for your product. *Sloan Management Review*. Retrieved from https://sloanreview.mit.edu/article/finding-the-right-job-for-your-product/

Covey, S., Merrill, A., & Merrill, R. (1994). *First things first*. New York, NY: Fireside.

Dintersmith, T. (2018). *What school could be*. Princeton, NJ: Princeton University Press.

Dworkin, D., & Spiegel, M. (2016, August 25). Leadership may not be the problem with your innovation team. *Harvard Business Review*. Retrieved from https://hbr.org/2016/08/leadership-may-not-be-the-problem-with-your-innovation-team

Dyer, J., Gregersen, H., & Christiansen, C. (2011). *The innovator's DNA*. Boston, MA: Harvard Business School.

Friedman, T. (2016). *Thank you for being late: An optimist's guide to thriving in the age of accelerations*. New York, NY: Farrar, Straus, and Giroux.

Gallagher, A., & Thordarson, K. (2018). *Design thinking for school leaders*. Alexandria, VA: Association for Supervision and Curriculum Development.

Godin, S. (2018). *This is marketing*. New York, NY: Portfolio/Penguin.

Gorbis, M. (2013). *The nature of the future: Dispatches from the socialstructed world*. New York, NY: Simon & Schuster.

Hamel, G., & Zanini, M. (2014, October). Build a change platform, not a change program. Retrieved from https://www.mckinsey.com/business-functions/organization/our-insights/build-a-change-platform-not-a-change-program

Hare, R., & Dillon, R. (2018). *The space: A guide for educators*. Irvine, CA: EdTech Press.

Hill, A., Mellon, L., Laker, B., & Goddard, J. (2016, October). The one type of leader who can turn around a failing school. *Harvard Business Review*. Retrieved from https://hbr .org/2016/10/the-one-type-of-leader-who-can-turn-around-a-failing-school

Institute for the Future. (2011). *Ecosystems of well-being in four futures map*. Retrieved from http://www.iftf.org/our-work/health-self/health-horizons/ecosystems-of-well-being/ecosystems-of-well-being-in-4-futures-map/

International Futures Forum. (n.d.). Three horizons. Retrieved from http://www .internationalfuturesforum.com/three-horizons

Jaruzelski, B., & Dehoff, K. (2010). How the top innovators keep winning. *strategy + business magazine*. Retrieved from https://www.strategyand.pwc.com/media/file/sb61_preprint _Global-Innov1000-10408.pdf

Kelley, D., & Kelley, T. (2013). *Creative confidence: Unleashing the creative potential within us all.* New York, NY: Random House.

Kelly, K. (2016). *The inevitable.* New York, NY: Penguin Press.

Kotter, J. (2016). *Our iceberg is melting.* New York, NY: Penguin Press.

Lafley, A., & Martin, R. (2013). *Playing to win.* Boston, MA: Harvard Business School Press.

Laloux, F. (2016). *Reinventing organizations.* Millis, MA: Nelson Parker.

Lehmann, C., & Chase, Z. (2015). *Building school 2.0: How to create the schools we need.* San Francisco, CA: Jossey-Bass.

Leonhard, G. (2016). *Technology vs humanity.* Switzerland: Fast Future.

Lichtman, G. (2014). *#EdJourney: A roadmap to the future of education.* San Francisco, CA: Jossey-Bass.

Lichtman, G. (2017). *Moving the rock: Seven levers we can press to transform education.* San Francisco, CA: Jossey-Bass.

Maslow, A. H. (1943). A theory of human motivation. *Psychological Review, 50*(4), 370–396.

McChrystal, S. (2015). *Team of teams: New rules of engagement for a complex world.* New York, NY: Penguin Random House.

Morris, L. (2011). *The innovation master plan.* Walnut Creek, CA: Innovation Academy.

Nichols, T. (2017). *The death of expertise.* New York, NY: Oxford University Press.

Pentland, A. (2014). *Social physics.* New York, NY: Penguin Press.

Porter, M. (1996, November-December). What is strategy? *Harvard Business Review.*

Putnam, R. (2015). *Our kids: The American dream in crisis.* New York, NY: Simon & Schuster.

Ravitch, D. (2010). *The Death and Life of the Great American School System: How Testing and Choice Are Undermining Education.* New York: Basic Books.

Ravitch, D. (2013). *Reign of Error: The Hoax of the Privatization Movement and the Danger to America's Public Schools.* New York: Knopf.

Ritchhart, R. (2015). *Creating cultures of thinking.* San Francisco, CA: Jossey-Bass.

Schleicher, A. (2018). *World Class: How to Build a 21st-Century School System.* Paris: OECD.

Socol, I., Moran, P., & Ratliff, C. (2018). *Timeless learning.* San Francisco, CA: Jossey-Bass.

Sull, D., & Eisenhardt, K. (2015). *Simple rules.* New York, NY: Houghton Mifflin Harcourt.

Sun T., & Cleary, T. (Trans.). (2003). *The art of war: Complete text and commentaries.* Boulder, CO: Shambhala.

Tucker, M. (Ed.) (2011). *Surpassing Shanghai: An Agenda for American Education Built on the World's Leading Systems.* Boston: Harvard Education Press.

Twenge, J. (2017). *iGen.* New York, NY: Atria.

Ulwick, A. (2016). *Jobs to be done.* Houston, TX: Idea Bite Press.

Whitman, G., & Kelleher, I. (2016). *Neuroteach: Brain science and the future of education.* Lanham, MD: Rowman and Littlefield.

Wilson, J. (2018). *The human side of changing education.* Thousand Oaks, CA: Corwin.

Zhao, Y. (2015). Globalization in Education. In J. D. Wright (Ed.), *International Encyclopedia of the Social and Behavioral Sciences (Second Edition)* (pp. 247–253). Amsterdam: Elsevier.

Zhao, Y. (2016, November 29). Stop Copying Others: TIMSS Lessons for America. Retrieved from http://zhaolearning.com/2016/11/30/stop-copying-others-timss-lessons-for-america/

Zhao, Y. (2017, September). The West and Asian Education: A Fatal Attraction. *New Internationalist*, 505, 24–25.

Zhao, Y. (2018). *What Works May Hurt: Side Effects in Education*. New York: Teachers College Press.

Zhao, Y. (2019). Side Effects in Education: Winners and Losers in School Voucher Programs. *Phi Delta Kappan, 100*(5), 63–66. Retrieved from https://journals.sagepub.com/doi/abs/10.1177/0031721719827553. doi:10.1177/0031721719827553

Zhao, Y., Emler, T., Snethen, A., & Yin, D. (2019). *From "Yes, But" to "Yes, And": Radical Changes in Education*. New York: Teachers College Press.

Zhao, Y., & Gearin, B. (2016). Squeezed Out. In *Creative Intelligence in the 21st Century* edited by D Ambrose, R. J. Sternberg, and J. S. Renzulli (pp. 121–138): N.P.: Springer.

Index

Leadership That Makes an Impact

LYN SHARRATT

Explore 14 essential parameters to guide system and school leaders toward building powerful collaborative learning cultures.

MICHAEL FULLAN

How do you break the cycle of surface-level change to tackle complex challenges? *Nuance* is the answer.

IAN JUKES & RYAN L. SCHAAF

The digital environment has radically changed how students need to learn. Get ready to be challenged to accommodate today's learners.

ERIC SHENINGER

Lead for efficacy in these disruptive times! Cultivating school culture focused on the achievement of students while anticipating change is imperative.

JOANNE MCEACHEN & MATTHEW KANE

Getting at the heart of what matters for students is key to deeper learning that connects with their lives.

LEE G. BOLMAN & TERRENCE E. DEAL

Sometimes all it takes to solve a problem is to reframe it by listening to wise advice from a trusted mentor.

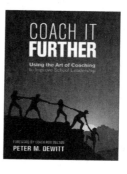

PETER M. DEWITT

This go-to guide is written for coaches, leaders looking to be coached, and leaders interested in coaching burgeoning leaders.

ANTHONY KIM & ALEXIS GONZALES-BLACK

Designed to foster flexibility and continuous innovation, this resource expands cutting-edge management and organizational techniques to empower schools with the agility and responsiveness vital to their new environment.

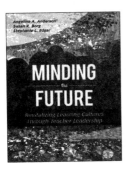

A SAGE Publishing Company

Helping educators make the greatest impact

CORWIN HAS ONE MISSION: to enhance education through intentional professional learning.

We build long-term relationships with our authors, educators, clients, and associations who partner with us to develop and continuously improve the best evidence-based practices that establish and support lifelong learning.